Tinker v. Des Moines:

Free speech for students

Meade Middle Media Center
1103 26th St.
Fort Meade, MD

UNDER·LAW

SUPREME COURT MILESTONES

Tinker v. Des Moines:

Free Speech for Students

SUSAN DUDLEY GOLD

Marshall Cavendish
Benchmark

New York

**To Jane Dudley Ruel, who allows her students the
freedom to think their own thoughts and encourages
them to express their own views**

*With special thanks to Professor David M. O'Brien of the
Woodrow Wilson Department of Politics at the University of
Virginia for reviewing the text of this book.*

Marshall Cavendish Benchmark
99 White Plains Road
Tarrytown, NY 10591
www.marshallcavendish.us

All Internet sites were available and accurate when sent to press.

Library of Congress Cataloging-in-Publication Data
Gold, Susan Dudley.
Tinker v. Des Moines : free speech for students / by Susan Dudley Gold.
p. cm. — (Supreme Court milestones)
Includes bibliographical references and index.
ISBN-13: 978-0-7614-2142-9 ISBN-10: 0-7614-2142-4
1. Tinker, John Frederick—Trials, litigation, etc.—Juvenile literature.
2. Des Moines Independent Community School District—Trials, litigation, etc.—
Juvenile literature. 3. Freedom of speech—United States—Juvenile literature. 4.
Students—Legal status, laws, etc.—United States—Juvenile literature. I. Title. II. Title:
Tinker versus Des Moines. III. Series.
KF228.T56G65 2006 342.7308'53—dc22 2005029838

Photo research by Candlepants Incorporated

The photographs in this book are used by permission and through the courtesy of: *AP
Wide World Photos*: 13, 65, 66, 67, 69. *Des Moines Register*: 17, 21, 27. *Corbis*: Bettmann,
30, 52, 73, 85, 102; Flip Schulke, 33. *Lyndon Baines Johnson Library*: 86. *Time-Life
Pictures/Getty Images*: 93, 95. *Jeffrey Sauger*: 105.

Series design by Sonia Chaghatzbanian
Printed in China
135642

contents

introduction

THE FIRST AMENDMENT

*Congress shall make no law respecting an establish-
ment of religion, or prohibiting the free exercise thereof;
or abridging the freedom of speech, or of the press; or the
right of the people peaceably to assemble, and to petition the Government for a redress of grievances.*

In 1965, as a growing number of Americans
began to question the wisdom of continuing to wage the
Vietnam War, three teenagers in Iowa defied the rules and
wore black armbands to school. They said they wore the
homemade bands to mourn the war's dead and to support
a cease-fire. That action ignited its own battle, one the
students and school officials would fight in the courts and
eventually take to the U.S. Supreme Court.

On February 24, 1969, the Court, in a 7 to 2 decision,
ruled that the students had a right to freely express their
views, under the protections granted in the First Amendment. As long as the students' actions did not disrupt
classes—and the Court ruled they did not—they had as
much right as adults to free speech.

The ruling in that case, *Tinker et al.* v. *Des Moines
Independent Community School District et al.*, has been
called "the broadest statement of students' rights" yet
rendered by the U.S. Supreme Court. In writing the

majority opinion in the case, Justice Abe Fortas intoned words that would echo loudly in every students' rights case to follow. "It can hardly be argued," he wrote, "that either students or teachers shed their constitutional rights to freedom of speech or expression at the schoolhouse gate."

STUDENTS' RIGHTS STANDARD

The ruling set a standard used to judge almost all other questions involving students' rights. In the years that followed the decision, school administrators, students, and courts referred to the *Tinker* case when deciding what limits, if any, should be applied to student newspapers, yearbooks, magazines, demonstrations, and other student activities. Even cases that involved student issues other than First Amendment rights relied on the words of Justice Fortas.

But more recent U.S. Supreme Court cases have put some limits on students' rights. A 1988 decision, in *Hazelwood School District* v. *Kuhlmeier*, allowed school officials to censor student newspaper articles as long as they had educational reasons to do so. In other cases, the Supreme Court has permitted educators to bar lewd and indecent speech and to punish students who use such words.

Some observers believe the Court's more conservative rulings regarding students' rights are a reaction to the serious problems schools face today. Mass shootings, drug use, and gang uprisings at schools have grabbed headlines since the days of the peaceful, silent armband protest.

Justice Hugo Black, one of two justices to dissent in the *Tinker* case, predicted that the decision would lead to chaos in the schools and a "new era of permissiveness." Today's schools have indeed become more open, although people disagree on whether that is good or bad. To critics, such permissiveness has led to violence, drug-related problems, and a decline in test scores. Others, however, believe schools encourage learning and teach important lessons about citizens' rights by being more open to student expression.

RIGHT TO SYMBOLIC SPEECH

The ruling also reconfirmed Americans' right to symbolic speech. The First Amendment protects free speech, but it does not define what types of speech are included in that guarantee. Unlike "pure speech"—which involves the spoken word—symbolic speech depends on actions or symbols to make its point. For example, protesters may burn an American flag in a symbolic gesture designed to express opposition to government policy. Such actions, however, lose their First Amendment protection if they present a clear and imminent threat of violence. If the protesters set the flag afire inside a crowded building, the Constitution would not protect such a dangerous act.

Even before Americans formed their own country, they relied on symbolic speech to make their views known. Enraged colonists burned King George in effigy to protest what they viewed as unfair taxes. Early U.S. Supreme Court opinions supported Americans' right to symbolic speech as long as it did not cause a "clear and present danger" to others. A 1940 decision in *Thornhill* v. *Alabama* ruled that the First Amendment protections extended to picketers as long as they did not destroy property or harm others. Three years later, the Court, in *West Virginia* v. *Barnette*, ruled that students also had a right to express themselves symbolically. In that case, students had remained silent while their classmates recited the Pledge of Allegiance. Their religious training as Jehovah's Witnesses required them to pledge loyalty only to God.

While the *Barnette* case focused on religious beliefs, *Tinker* v. *Des Moines* expanded the First Amendment protection of symbolic speech to other types of views as well. The Court allowed students the right to symbolic speech within the schools, however, only as long as their actions did not disrupt classes. In crafting the *Tinker* decision, Justice Fortas noted that it would clearly be unconstitutional to forbid students to talk about their opposition to the Vietnam War. Banning "the silent, passive 'witness of the armbands,'" he wrote, would be "no less offensive to the Constitution's guarantees."

one
WAR IN VIETNAM, CONFLICT IN AMERICA

In February 1965, under orders from President Lyndon B. Johnson, U.S. bombers targeted North Vietnam in a military mission known as Operation Rolling Thunder. The first American combat troops arrived in South Vietnam the following month. By December 1965 the United States had become embroiled in a war in Southeast Asia that would ultimately claim the lives of 58,200 U.S. soldiers and millions of Vietnamese soldiers and civilians.

Soon after the first bombings, Americans who opposed U.S. involvement in the hostilities between North and South Vietnam began expressing their views at marches, in letters to the editor, and through other acts of protest. As criticism of America's role in the war increased, so, too, did the number of demonstrations. In October 1965 protesters held events in forty U.S. cities.

On college campuses and elsewhere, some protests turned violent. Three people set themselves on fire in 1965 to protest the war, including an eighty-two-year-old woman and a young Quaker father. Young men burned their draft cards. College students took over buildings and advocated violent tactics to block government military efforts. The violence associated with these protests and the links to radical groups turned many Americans away from the antiwar message.

At the end of 1965, more than 184,000 American forces were stationed in Vietnam. By then, 636 U.S. soldiers had been killed in combat. Few American communities escaped the war's effects. As fighting became more intense, more and more hometowns mourned for young men killed in the jungles of Southeast Asia. Emotions ran high between those who responded to the deaths by defending the administration's course (hawks) and those who called for peace (doves). Supporters of the war quickly adopted such slogans as "America, Love It or Leave It," which questioned the loyalty of those who opposed the conflict. In some circles, anyone who spoke out against the war was considered a traitor. Questioning the administration's policies, they believed, amounted to aiding and abetting America's foes. The peace movement, and those who supported it, threatened the stability and security of the nation, these citizens warned.

This did not deter Americans who thought the country should not be fighting a war in Southeast Asia. "Victory in a war such as the United States is waging in Vietnam would demean our country more than defeat," a writer in *The Nation* contended in 1965. Believing it was their patriotic duty to oppose the war, these Americans created their own slogans ("War is not healthy for children and other living things" was one) and held demonstrations for peace.

MARCH ON WASHINGTON

On November 27, 1965, between twenty-five thousand to thirty-five thousand Americans participated in a peace march in Washington, D.C., to protest U.S. involvement in the war in Vietnam. Organized by the National Committee for a Sane Nuclear Policy (SANE), the march attracted thousands of middle-class Americans, some pushing baby carriages and walking with their older children. According to a report in the next day's *New York Times*,

IN 1965, PRESIDENT LYNDON BAINES JOHNSON AUTHORIZED THE BOMBING OF
NORTH VIETNAM. ON NOVEMBER 5, A U.S. B-52 DROPPED A LOAD OF 750 LB.
BOMBS ON THE COUNTRY.

families and adults "far outnumbered" student groups and radical left sympathizers. The Women's International League for Peace and Freedom and the American Friends Service Committee, a Quaker organization, were among the groups participating in the march. SANE coordinated the event with a goal of keeping the demonstration "restrained and responsible." Coretta Scott King, wife of civil rights leader, the Reverend Dr. Martin Luther King Jr., spoke at the gathering, urging an end to hostilities. "Freedom and destiny in America," she told the crowd, "are bound together with freedom and justice in Vietnam."

Among those attending the march were two mothers from Des Moines, Iowa, Lorena Jeanne Tinker and Margaret Eckhardt. Both had brought along their teenage sons, John Tinker and Christopher Eckhardt. Mrs. Tinker's husband, the Reverend Leonard Tinker, a Methodist minister, headed the peace education program for the American Friends Service Committee. Both Tinkers had long been active in liberal causes. Margaret Eckhardt attended the peace rally in her role as president of the Des Moines chapter of the Women's International League for Peace and Freedom. The boys, both fifteen, rode the bus to Washington, D.C., with their mothers and other protesters. Also on board were members of the Students for a Democratic Society (SDS), a left-leaning student group active on college campuses.

Participating in a march with so many other people with similar views had an impact on the boys. John Tinker later recalled how impressed he was that so many people opposed the Vietnam War. "The main impression of being in that crowd in D.C. was the realization of the vast numbers of people who thought that the U.S. should not be in Vietnam," he said. "I had never seen so many people together in one place before."

Although President Lyndon B. Johnson had said he believed Americans had the right to criticize foreign policy, a few bystanders tried to grab the banners of a radical group participating in the march. Only that one minor skirmish between marchers and counterprotesters was reported by the *New York Times* during the otherwise peaceful demonstration.

On the bus ride home, the boys joined a discussion on what to do next. Among the suggestions made during the trip was that protesters could wear black armbands as a sign of their opposition to the Vietnam War. A number of Des Moines peace advocates met at the Eckhardts' house on December 11, 1965, to discuss the subject further. Christopher Eckhardt and several other members of the local Unitarian Church's Liberal Religious Youth Group attended the meeting.

North Vietnamese forces fighting in the south had agreed to a twelve-hour truce during the Christmas holidays. On December 9, 1965, U.S. Senator Robert F. Kennedy had proposed that the United States extend the cease-fire indefinitely. By the end of the meeting at the Eckhardts' home, the group had decided to support peace efforts on the three college campuses in the area (Drake, Grinnell, and Iowa State). The college students at the meeting agreed to recruit fellow students to wear black armbands on December 16. They would wear the bands until the end of the year for two reasons: to mourn American and Vietnamese dead killed in the war, and to show support for Senator Kennedy's cease-fire proposal.

The group called a press conference later that day to announce the planned college protest with the hope of attracting national support. The local television station broadcast the announcement on its 10 pm news show. A small item in the Des Moines *Sunday Register* also detailed the plan.

STUDENTS EMBRACE PLAN

Several of the high school students and at least one junior high student decided that they would participate in the peace effort as well. Ross Peterson, who attended the meeting and was a student at Theodore Roosevelt High School, wrote an article about the armband protest for the student newspaper. In it, he told of the plan to don armbands on December 16. He also told students of a meeting planned on New Year's Eve at a student's house to discuss the war. The article concluded with the words: "All students interested in saving lives and ending the war in Vietnam are urged to attend [the New Year's meeting]."

When Peterson showed the article to the newspaper adviser, he was told that school administrators would have to approve it before it could be published.

The story—titled "We Mourn/Attention Students!"—immediately caused concern among school officials. They told Peterson the story would not be published in the school paper. In addition, principals of Des Moines' five high schools and other school officials met on December 14 to discuss the students' planned protest. At the meeting, they concluded that the students' action might disrupt classes and decided to ban the armbands. During testimony at the district court trial several months later, E. Raymond Peterson, director of secondary education in Des Moines, said the principals adopted the ban not because they objected to the students' views on the Vietnam War but because they believed demonstrations did not belong in the schools.

The following day, the *Des Moines Register* reported on the upcoming student protest and the principals' ban. In the front-page article, E. Raymond Peterson (no relation to student Ross Peterson) expressed concern that the armband protest would disrupt classes. "The

As soon as Chris Eckhardt arrived at Roosevelt High School in Des Moines, Iowa, wearing a black armband in protest against the Vietnam War, he walked to the principal's office. He knew he was breaking the rules, but he did not expect the harsh reception he received there.

schools are no place for demonstrations," he told the reporter. "We allow for free discussion of these things in classes." Peterson added that the principals had decided to ban the armbands because of a school policy forbidding "anything that is a disturbing situation within the school." He dismissed the student protest as unimportant, calling it an attempt by "eight or 10 students" to "get publicity" for their cause.

That day, too, school officials announced to students that they would not be allowed to wear black armbands as a protest against the war. The year before, students had been encouraged to wear black armbands to school to "mourn" the death of school spirit. School officials had approved of that action, but they believed that wearing armbands to mourn those killed in Vietnam might spark controversy.

News of the planned demonstration sparked strong objections from some teachers and students. According to Christopher Eckhardt, the gym coach at Roosevelt High warned protesters not to come to class wearing armbands and likened them to Communist sympathizers. Mary Beth Tinker said her math teacher spent the December 15 lesson discussing Vietnam War protesters and threatened to bar students who wore armbands from his classroom.

Despite such opposition and the new rule against armbands, more than two dozen students wore black arm-bands to school on December 16 and 17. Most attended high school, but a few, like Mary Beth, Hope, and Paul Tinker, were elementary and middle school students. On the first day of the protest, Christopher Eckhardt wore his black armband over his jacket and headed for Roosevelt High School, where he was a sophomore. As soon as he arrived, he went to the principal's office, aware that he was breaking the rules by wearing the armband. In the hallway, a few students threatened him, and the captain of the school's football team tried to rip off the black cloth.

At the principal's office, officials pressured Christopher to remove the armband. The vice principal asked him, "Do you want a busted nose?" The school's guidance counselor told him that his actions might jeopardize his chances of getting into a good college after high school. Under such pressure, Christopher broke down in tears, but he continued to refuse to remove the armband. At that point, the vice principal called Christopher's mother, but Margaret Eckhardt supported her son's right to protest. Christopher, who had served as president of the student council in elementary and junior high school, believed he had a constitutional right to express his views in this way. Rather than take off the armband, he defied the vice principal's orders and was suspended from school. Officials also suspended two other Roosevelt High students, Christine Singer, a sophomore, and Bruce Clark, a senior. Clark, like Eckhardt, belonged to the Liberal Religious Youth Group.

John and Mary Beth Tinker had fashioned their armbands from black cloth they had found among their mother's sewing supplies. Mary Beth, thirteen, wore her armband to class at Warren Harding Junior High School. At first, her action attracted little attention. Some students questioned her about her action; a few teachers looked at the armband but said nothing about it. When Mary Beth went to her afternoon math class, however, the math teacher who had expressed his opposition to such protests the day before sent her to the principal's office. The vice principal told her to take off the band, which she did, and allowed her to go back to class. However, the girls' adviser, Vera Tarmann, called her out of class a second time and suspended her for violating school rules.

John Tinker decided not to wear his armband until the second day of the protest, December 17. In explaining his reasons for delay to the district court judge later, John said, "I didn't feel that I should just wear it [the armband] against the will of the principals of the high schools without even trying to talk to them first." On December 16, after the first suspensions, the students called Ora Niffenegger, the school board's president, to ask the board to hold a special meeting to discuss the issue. Niffenegger declined. John read the local newspaper's account of Niffenegger's comments in which the school board's president treated the armband protests as a "trivial" matter. Upset that the official had refused to at least give the students a hearing on the matter, John wore his armband the next day when he went to North High School, where he was a junior.

John's protest elicited comments from some students, both pro and con. Unlike the football player who threatened Eckhardt, a member of the North High School football team defended Tinker's right to express his views. Teachers either did not notice his armband or chose not to respond to it. Eventually, an office staff member saw John's armband and reported it to the principal, who called him into his office. Given the choice of taking off the armband or leaving the school, John went home with his father. Rather than formally suspending John, the principal told the young protester that he could return to class and would not lose credits if he did not wear the armband in the future.

The two youngest Tinker children, Hope, an eleven-year-old fifth-grader, and Paul, who was eight and in the first grade, encountered no difficulties when they wore black armbands to James Madison Elementary School. Teachers in both elementary classes led students in a discussion about the protest, without punishing the two young armband wearers. The rule against armbands did not extend to elementary schools.

MARY BETH TINKER GOT IN TROUBLE WITH HER MATH TEACHER WHEN SHE
WORE A BLACK ARMBAND TO SCHOOL IN PROTEST AGAINST THE VIETNAM WAR.

A stormy meeting

Des Moines schools were scheduled to close on the following Thursday, December 23, for the Christmas holiday. School board members prepared for a discussion of the armband issue at the board's regular meeting, set for Tuesday, December 21. It promised to be quite a battle.

After school officials suspended their children, the Tinkers and the Eckhardts asked the Iowa chapter of the American Civil Liberties Union (ACLU) to look into the matter. Founded in 1920, the ACLU is the nation's major defender of civil rights. The organization took a lead role in the cases that led to school desegregation, defended Jehovah's Witness students whose religion did not permit them to say the pledge to the American flag, and represented John Scopes, the teacher on trial for discussing evolution, among others. In response to the parents' request, Craig Sawyer agreed to take on the students' case for the Iowa Civil Liberties Union (ICLU). Sawyer, an assistant professor at Drake Law School in Des Moines, would represent the students at the upcoming school board meeting.

After the ICLU's press release on the matter, school superintendent Dwight Davis announced that officials had acted because they feared the protests would disrupt the schools, not because they wanted to deprive students of their rights. Ora Niffenegger, president of the school board, said that he was "absolutely opposed to this type of demonstration within the confines of the school."

Over the weekend, members of the American Friends Service Committee and other peace groups met to rally supporters in preparation for the school board meeting. Sunday's *Des Moines Register* ran an editorial supporting the students' right to express their views peacefully and encouraged the students and their parents to negotiate a settlement with school authorities.

A front-page story in Monday's *Des Moines Register* detailed the upcoming meeting and recapped the controversy. The meeting the next day would be the school board's first opportunity to review the ban and take a stand on the school officials' actions regarding the student protest. By the time school board president Niffenegger called the meeting to order on Tuesday afternoon, 200 people had crammed into the room to hear the board's discussion of the armband situation. Many in the audience wore black armbands to show their support of the students. The *New York Times* followed the events and reported the details to readers throughout the nation.

During the often contentious discussion that followed, ICLU attorney Sawyer demanded that the school board lift the students' suspensions and allow the armbands. The students, he said, had "an absolute right to disobey a ruling that is unconstitutional."

Two school board members expressed support for the students' position. The Reverend L. Robert Keck, a Methodist minister and board member, said that he believed the rule banning the armbands should be overturned. "Banning controversial activity harms education," Keck stated. Board member Arthur Davis, too, spoke against the ban. The students' actions, he said, did not create a "clear and present danger" to order at the schools.

Several students spoke at the meeting, some urging the board members to overrule the ban, while others opposed the protest and supported the administration.

One student, Dean Stonehaker, told the board that the coach at Roosevelt High School had led students in chanting "Beat the Viet Cong." The coach, Donald Prior, had also accused students who did not shout the chant of being "pinkos or Communists," according to Stonehaker. Some of the protesters had reported earlier that they had been threatened, kicked, or hit by other students for wearing the armbands.

Both Davis and Keck argued that those causing the disruption—not the protesters—should be punished. "We have been intimidated by the threat of violence," said Keck, "and have thus allowed the ruffian element to determine educational policies."

Davis said he viewed the students' armband protest as "a clear issue of an individual's constitutional right of free expression." The father of one of the suspended protesters also addressed the issue of freedom of speech. "No subject of general interest is so taboo that we cannot tolerate free discussion," said Bud Singer, whose daughter Christine had been among the suspended Roosevelt High protesters.

Niffenegger, the board's president, had already stated his position in newspaper stories on the controversy so when he opposed the protest, it came as no surprise. Two other board members, George Caudill and Merle Schlampp, spoke in support of the school ban during the meeting. Caudill repeated the school officials' concern that the armband protest would disrupt classes. Schlampp argued that school authorities, not students, had to be in control of the schools.

Ron Cohen, president of the student council at Roosevelt High, told the board that he believed the protest was "detrimental to education" because of the controversy it had created. A man who had served in the military during World War II said the schools—like the military—should operate under strict discipline. The veteran, Merle Emerson, said students who violated school rules should be punished.

For two hours, board members, school officials, and people in the audience, including Lorena Tinker, spoke on the issue. Emotions ran high as speakers voiced their views. Finally, board member John Haydon proposed that the board put off deciding the matter until its next meeting in January. At that, professor Sawyer erupted. "I demand that you decide now," he shouted. The board, he continued, should not "ignore the children's plight."

Haydon and the three board members who had spoken against the student protest ignored the plea and voted in favor of the motion to postpone. Board member Mary Grefe joined the two members who had supported the students—Keck and Davis—in voting against the postponement.

As soon as the vote to table the matter had been cast, college students from Iowa State University began picketing outside the building. The student group, members of the antiwar Students for a Democratic Society, raised signs reading "Controversy belongs in school" and "Freedom means free speech." According to a report in the *New York Times*, some of the students who had been suspended for wearing armbands at Des Moines schools joined in the picket line.

Sawyer said school authorities had violated the students' constitutional right to free speech and added that the matter might end up in court.

Home for the Holidays

Two days after the board meeting, school in Des Moines closed for the holidays. The controversy over the student protest subsided somewhat while the community celebrated Christmas and students enjoyed a break from school. Mary Beth Tinker, however, remembers a not-so-merry holiday season that year. A few people took violent steps to denounce the students' school protest. A man threatened Leonard Tinker on a radio show. Someone threw red paint on the Tinker house. Even more frightening, a woman telephoned Mary Beth and threatened to kill her. And on Christmas Eve, the family got a call from someone who said their house would be blown up by the next morning. The thirteen-year-old felt the impact of such threats. "I realized how hateful, how irrational people could be," said Mary Beth many years later. "Subconsciously there was a part of me that withdrew."

That Christmas Eve in Vietnam, U.S. and Vietnamese soldiers honored the truce agreed to earlier by both sides. On December 26, however, the Viet Cong—North Vietnamese forces in South Vietnam—resumed attacks. Two days later, the United States sent its B-52 bombers on air raids targeting the Viet Cong in Quang Tri Province north of Saigon, the capital of South Vietnam. The cease-fire continued in North Vietnam, mainly because American and South Vietnamese leaders hoped to persuade the North Vietnamese to agree to negotiations aimed at ending the war.

The effort failed, and on January 7, 1966, American soldiers launched the largest U.S. operation of the war to date. Almost eight thousand U.S. troops participated in Operation Crimp, with the goal of capturing Viet Cong headquarters in the Saigon region. The campaign targeted the Viet Cong's vast tunnel system but was unsuccessful in routing out the enemy base.

On Monday, January 3, Des Moines schools reopened. None of the suspended students wore their armbands to school that day. Christopher Eckhardt and Mary Beth and John Tinker chose to stay home from school until the school board made a final ruling on the issue. The two other students suspended in the controversy, Christine Singer and Bruce Clark, chose to take off the armbands and attend classes.

That evening the school board faced another large crowd packed into the hearing room. The arguments resumed much as before. A majority of the speakers from

MARY BETH TINKER'S MOTHER (RIGHT) WAS AN EARLY PROTESTER AGAINST THE VIETNAM WAR.

the audience supported the students' position. Among them were representatives of the Women's International League for Peace and Freedom, the Iowa Civil Liberties Union, professors from the local colleges, and members of the Eckhardt and Tinker families. Christopher Eckhardt, in his comments to the board, noted that the school officials' ban, not the armband protest itself, caused "quite a disturbance in the community." His father, William, also shared his views on the matter. Obeying rules without question, he noted, was the same kind of behavior "so greatly admired in Nazi Germany."

After a dozen or so speeches, the board members cast their votes on the ban. As expected, the four members who had favored postponing a decision at the last meeting voted this time to uphold the ban on student armbands. They were joined by member Mary Grefe. Keck and Davis voted against the policy.

TWO
STUDENTS GO TO COURT

THE DAY AFTER THE SCHOOL BOARD'S VOTE,
John and Mary Beth Tinker and Christopher Eckhardt
returned to school without armbands. Instead, they wore
black clothing as a sign of their continuing protest. As
Christopher Eckhardt and several others had noted at the
board meeting, the protest had gone beyond the Vietnam
War and now embraced the free-speech rights of students.

The Eckhardts and the Tinkers discussed the situation
with the Iowa Civil Liberties Union and decided to pursue
the matter in court. "The school board was trying to suppress and did suppress the expression of our ideas," John
Tinker said later in explaining why the families went to
court. In a speech he gave at Roosevelt High—Eckhardt's
old school—in 1995, Tinker said, "I was sure we were
right. We'd been taught about the Constitution and I was
sure we had the right [to wear the armbands]."

Louise Noun, chairman of the ICLU, volunteered to
help finance the court fight. The organization asked Dan
L. Johnston to represent the students in the court case.
His firm had handled civil rights cases before for the
ICLU. Just a year out of law school, Johnston eagerly
accepted the assignment. "The school board in my
opinion did not have sufficient justification to suspend
the students," said Johnston later.

MARY BETH AND JOHN TINKER HOLD UP THEIR CONTROVERSIAL ARMBANDS.

A CASE OF RIGHTS DENIED

On March 14, 1966, the young lawyer filed the students' claim in Iowa's U.S. District Court. The suit listed as plaintiffs Mary Beth and John Tinker and Christopher Eckhardt as well as their fathers, Leonard Tinker and William Eckhardt, as "next friends," because the students were minors. Johnston filed the suit against the school district, the school board members, the superintendent, the five principals, the director of education, math teacher Richard Moberly, girls' adviser Vera Tarmann, and several other school officials.

In his arguments, Johnston contended that the students had "lawfully and peacefully engaged in the exercise of the right of free speech secured for them by Amendments One and Fourteen of the United States Constitution." In banning the armbands, Johnston argued, the school board had deprived his clients of their rights. The First Amendment guarantees the right to free speech, while the Fourteenth Amendment directs the states not to deprive anyone of "life, liberty, or property, without due process of law." In addition, the amendment specifically forbids the states from limiting citizens' "privileges or immunities," rights such as free speech that are included in the Bill of Rights.

Johnston also claimed that, under federal law, the board should be found liable for violating a person's legal rights. If the court did not order the board to allow the armbands, Johnston said, the ban would cause the students "irreparable harm" and force them to pursue "vexatious, expensive, annoying litigation."

Johnston asked the court to rescind the ban against the armbands and also to award the students one dollar in damages because of the "injuries" caused by the board's action. The students' "injuries" resulted from their suspension from school: They missed out on classwork and received a bad mark on their school record, endured "mental anguish [and] embarrassment," and were deprived of their rights. Johnston included the reference to federal law and the request for a penalty to ensure that the case would not be dismissed if the students graduated from high school before the case had been settled.

Allan Herrick filed the school board's reply on April 29. In his defense of the school board, he maintained that the students wore armbands to school "in direct violations of the reasonable rules" adopted to maintain order at the schools. Allowing students to continue violating the rules, Herrick said, would have "threatened a breakdown in the discipline and orderly conduct" in the classrooms.

Before the trial began, the Fifth Circuit in Mississippi ruled on a similar case. In that situation, a principal at an all-black public school in Philadelphia, Mississippi, suspended students who wore "freedom buttons" as a protest against racial segregation. The students took the case to court, claiming that the principal's action violated their free-speech rights. The three-judge panel ruled unanimously that students had the right to wear symbols to express their views as long as they did not "materially and substantially interfere with the requirements of appropriate discipline in the operation of the school." Judge Walter Gewin, author of the opinion, warned that when students' actions did not cause a substantial disruption, school officials could not "infringe on their right to free and unrestricted expression as guaranteed to them under the First Amendment to the Constitution." Johnston would use the ruling in the case, *Burnside* v. *Byars*, to bolster his own arguments.

On the same day the *Burnside* decision was issued, the Fifth Circuit issued an opposite ruling in another case, *Blackwell* v. *Issaquena County Board of Education*, also involving students' right to wear political buttons. This

PROTESTS WERE RAMPANT THROUGHOUT THE NATION DURING THE 1960S. CIVIL RIGHTS MARCHERS IN MISSISSIPPI WORE "FREEDOM BUTTONS" TO PROTEST AGAINST SEGREGATION. THAT CASE WENT TO COURT BEFORE THE TINKERS' CASE WAS HEARD.

time, however, school officials proved that the school had a history of racial violence, that students wearing the buttons harassed others who did not, and that the buttons heightened racial tension at the school.

In the Witness Chair

The two sides in the *Tinker* case met in Chief Judge Roy L. Stephenson's courtroom in Des Moines on July 25, 1966. As in many civil cases, the judge would decide the case without a jury. During the all-day session, the three students told their story. John Tinker testified first. He answered Johnston's questions, then replied to questions from attorney Philip Lovrien, who represented the school board along with Allan Herrick.

Mary Beth followed her brother to the witness chair. Both gave straightforward answers on their actions leading up to and during the protest, their reasons for taking part, and the results of their decision to wear the armbands to school.

Johnston and Lovrien both questioned Christopher Eckhardt longer than anyone else. Christopher described his day at school step by step, detailing his decision to report to the principal's office, the teasing and threats of other students, the comments of school officials, and his ultimate suspension. More than thirty years later, Eckhardt related his testimony about the vice principal's question on the day he wore the armband, "Do you want a busted nose?" He recalled seeing the vice principal walk out of the courtroom during that part of the testimony. "I still don't know whether it was out of shame" or that he just had to use the restroom, Eckhardt said.

All three students strongly denied that parents or anyone else had pressured them into participating in the armband protest.

Seven other witnesses testified that day, all school

employees or officials connected to the school district. The principal at North High School, attended by John Tinker, and the vice principals at Roosevelt High, Eckhardt's school, and Warren Harding Junior High, where Mary Beth Tinker was a student, gave their accounts of the armband incidents at their schools. Mary Beth's mathematics teacher and the girls' adviser who suspended her also testified, as did the president of the school board, Ora Niffenegger. None of these witnesses recounted any specific violent acts resulting from the armband protest.

A memo provided to the court by E. Raymond Peterson, director of secondary education, spelled out the reasons for the ban. It stated that the principals supported the ban on armbands because:

• Memorial Day or Veterans Day ceremonies offered a better place to mourn war dead;

• Allowing armbands might lead to displays of other, more objectionable symbols such as the Nazi Iron Cross;

• Such a demonstration might inflame students who knew soldiers who had died in Vietnam and that could lead to violence;

• Students are captive audiences who should not be forced to witness such protests, supported by only a few;

• The ban was the proper method, under school rules, to deal with the situation.

In closing arguments the next day, Johnston commented on the hypocrisy of a school policy that allowed

PRESERVING AND PROTECTING AMERICA'S LIBERTIES

Before the American Civil Liberties Union began its push to protect individual rights, no one had ever won a free-speech case before the U.S. Supreme Court. Since its founding in 1920, the organization has stood against governmental abuses of power and for individual rights. In its quest to guard Americans' freedoms, the ACLU has represented thousands of clients seeking to secure their rights in courts throughout the country. The group's first big trial occurred in 1925 when the ACLU hired famed defense attorney Clarence Darrow to defend biology teacher John Scopes's right to teach evolution to his students. A jury convicted Scopes of violating Tennessee law and fined him, but the Tennessee Supreme Court, while upholding the law, threw out Scopes's conviction on technical grounds.

That same year, the ACLU lost one of its earliest U.S. Supreme Court cases, *Gitlow* v. *New York*, but won an important concession from the Court. The decision acknowledged that the Fourteenth Amendment protected freedom of speech and of the press from the control of the states. Such freedoms, according to the opinion, "are among the fundamental personal rights and 'liberties' protected by the due process clause of the Fourteenth Amendment from impairment by the state."

The ACLU's mission is to preserve and protect the individual rights guaranteed to Americans by the U.S. Constitution, with an emphasis on those freedoms specified in the Bill of Rights. Originally called the Civil Liberties Bureau, the organization was founded by Crystal Eastman, a graduate of Vassar who studied law at New York University and lobbied for workers' rights and the right of women to vote, and Roger Baldwin, a sociology teacher, Harvard graduate, and pacifist. Both Eastman and Baldwin had taken stands against U.S. involvement in World War I. Eastman edited an antiwar journal and served as a leader in the Women's Peace Party, which opposed the war. Baldwin led the American Union Against Militarism, which defended conscientious objectors and those resisting the draft. The organization was a precursor of the Civil Liberties Bureau and the ACLU. Baldwin himself served nine months in jail after refusing to be drafted into the service in 1918.

On January 19, 1920, New York awarded the ACLU its first charter. Among the organization's first members were social activist Jane Addams, future U.S. Supreme Court Justice Felix Frankfurter, and Helen Keller, who overcame deafness and blindness to become a noted lecturer and writer. The board adopted a policy to defend freedom of speech among other civil liberties, regardless of the content of the speech.

Several early leaders in the ACLU had ties to the Communist Party. In 1940, after becoming disillusioned with the party, Baldwin led a controversial and ultimately successful campaign within the organization to remove all communists from the ACLU board. As a result, Elizabeth Gurley Flynn, a strongly opinionated and dedicated Communist, lost her seat on the board. To many, the removal represented the organization's "most regrettable departure from its own principles." Despite this action, however, the ACLU continued to support the right of Communists to free speech and other liberties.

During its long history, the ACLU has been intimately involved in almost every important civil liberties court case. These battles have included many controversial clients from both sides of the political spectrum. In 1950, during the anti-Communist hysteria fostered by Senator

Joseph McCarthy, the ACLU unsuccessfully challenged the U.S. government's requirement that union leaders file affidavits stating they were not Communists. Almost three decades later, in 1978, the organization won a case on behalf of the leader of a neo-Nazi group whose right to hold a demonstration was denied by the town of Skokie, Illinois. The Illinois Supreme Court ruled that the town's actions violated the First Amendment, and the U.S. Supreme Court refused to overturn the lower court's decision.

Among the many landmark Supreme Court cases in which the ACLU has participated are the following:

• 1943: *Hirabayashi* v. *United States*. Represented Japanese Americans who had been forced to move from the West Coast and interned in prison camps after the Japanese attack on Pearl Harbor. The ACLU argued that the policy was unconstitutional and racially discriminatory, but the Court accepted the government's claims that the internment was militarily necessary.

• 1943: *West Virginia* v. *Barnette*. The Court agreed with the ACLU position that the children of Jehovah's Witnesses should not be forced to say the Pledge of Allegiance to the U.S. flag because it violated their freedom of religion.

• 1954: *Brown* v. *Board of Education*. Filed an *amicus* brief in support of Brown and desegregation of public schools. The Court agreed and ruled that segregating school children based on race was unconstitutional.

• 1961: *Mapp* v. *Ohio*. Represented Dollree Mapp in her appeal of a conviction based on evidence illegally seized from her house. The Court ruled that evidence gained from such unconstitutional searches and seizures could not be used in court against a defendant.

• 1962: *Engel* v. *Vitale*. Successfully argued that schools could not lead students in prayer in violation of the First Amendment's ban on a state religion.

• 1971: *New York Times* v. *United States*. Called "the greatest freedom of the press confrontation in American history," the case argued by the ACLU resulted in the publication of the Pentagon Papers, a secret report on U.S. failures in conducting the war in Vietnam. The decision undermined President Richard M. Nixon's claims of national security and confirmed the importance of open debate and access to information in a democracy.

• 1973: *Doe* v. *Bolton*. The companion case to *Roe* v. *Wade* that established a woman's right to an abortion.

• 1997: *Reno* v. *ACLU*. The Court gave unanimous approval to the ACLU position that the Communications Decency Act banning "indecency" on the Internet was unconstitutional. It was one of the most stunning wins for civil liberties in the 1990s.

• 2003: Several cases challenging the right of the U.S. government to imprison suspected terrorists without filing charges against them or allowing them to consult attorneys. The Supreme Court ruled that citizens and others held without charges or trial were being denied constitutional rights. The Court ordered the government to allow the detainees to consult lawyers and have hearings to review the charges against them.

In 2005, the ACLU has branches in all fifty states. The organization's more than sixty lawyers work with two thousand volunteer lawyers on about six thousand cases each year. It participates in more U.S. Supreme Court cases than any other organization except the U.S. Department of Justice. In addition, the ACLU sponsors educational and lobbying programs focusing on a number of civil liberties topics, including AIDS, lesbian and gay rights, voting rights, and women's and workers' rights.

While ACLU positions often attract criticism, especially from conservative groups, the organization does not back away from controversy. "Historically, the people whose opinions are the most controversial or extreme are the people whose rights are most often threatened," the ACLU Web site notes. "Once the government has the power to violate one person's rights, it can use that power against everyone. We work to stop the erosion of civil liberties before it's too late."

students to wear political buttons and Nazi insignia while at the same time banning armbands worn to mourn those killed in Vietnam. He also noted that the students had not disrupted classes or caused any disturbances at the schools.

Lovrien and Herrick both spoke for the school board. Lovrien argued that schools existed to provide education, not as a forum for protests. School officials, he said, had to be allowed to adopt reasonable rules to maintain order. Herrick noted that the students had participated in the protest knowing full well that such activity violated school rules. Their punishment, and the ban itself, should stand, he told the judge.

A Ruling and an Appeal

Five and a half weeks later, on September 1, Judge Stephenson issued his ruling. The school board, he said, had the authority to ban the students' armbands even though the protest did not substantially disrupt the schools. The ban fell under the board's power to set rules for student behavior. According to the judge, the school board took "reasonable" measures to enforce school discipline and prevent disturbances when it prohibited the armbands. He ruled that school officials should be "given a wide discretion" to take action to prevent disturbances that they had reason to anticipate. In making his decision, Stephenson noted but ignored the Fifth Circuit's previous ruling in *Burnside* v. *Byars*. He did, however, accept Johnston's argument that wearing armbands was a form of expression and as such fell under the definition of free speech in the First Amendment. Johnston would use that concession to further the students' cause in future courts.

Undeterred by Stephenson's ruling, Johnston appealed the case to the Court of Appeals for the Eighth Circuit. A panel composed of three of the eight appeals judges reviewed the evidence presented at the district court trial, considered the briefs, and weighed the arguments presented by both sides. In April 1967, the three attorneys recapped their arguments for the appeals judges during a hearing in St. Louis, Missouri. This time, no witnesses gave testimony. Unable to reach a decision in the case, the panel of judges passed the matter to the full court of appeals.

In October, the lawyers once again argued their case. Johnston focused on the argument that the school board had deprived his clients of the constitutional right of free speech. Lovrien and Herrick reiterated their position that school officials should be able to make reasonable rules to maintain order in the schools. "If courts continue second-guessing [school] administrators and tell them what to do and not to do," Lovrien told the court, "I think we're in for a lot of administration by courts and not by the schools."

In the end, the court could not reach a decision. The judges divided equally on the appeal with a 4 to 4 vote. Under the rules of the court, that meant the district court's decision remained intact. On November 3, 1967, the appeals court issued only a one-paragraph statement that merely recited the appeal and noted that the lower court's ruling would stand.

The outcome surprised Johnston, who believed the students had a strong case. "I thought it was an easy case and that we would win . . . in the federal district court," Johnston said in an article on the landmark case thirty years later. John Tinker, too, had thought the lower courts would rule in their favor. "I felt from the beginning that we were right, and that we would win. Later I was not so sure we would win, but I still thought we were right," he said during an online session arranged by the American Bar Association.

The fact that the rulings went against the students, however, meant that they would have the chance to plead their case before the highest court in the nation. "Fortunately, looking back, we did lose at the lower court level," Christopher Eckhardt said in a 1999 discussion about the case, "because if we had won there, this case could never have become such a landmark decision."

THREE
MAKING A CASE

AS THE *Tinker* case SLOWLY WOUND ITS WAY through the court system, the three students whose protest had spurred the legal action were growing up. By the time the Eighth Circuit Court ruled on their appeal, Christopher Eckhardt was a high school senior, John Tinker had graduated, and Mary Beth Tinker had begun her sophomore year.

After the appeals court issued its ruling allowing the lower court decision to stand, Johnston turned his sights to the next step in the appeals process. The students had one last shot at winning their case—in the highest court of the land, the U.S. Supreme Court.

To win a spot on the Supreme Court's docket, a case must address one of three issues: constitutional rights or questions, rulings by different courts that conflict with each other, or a decision by a state court on a federal law. The Supreme Court hears only a small portion of the thousands of cases submitted for review each year. Most of the time, lawyers file a petition with the Court requesting that their case be heard and outlining why the Court should consider it. This is called a petition for *certiorari* (meaning "to be informed of"). If the court grants *certiorari*, the records of the case are transferred from the lower courts to the Supreme Court, so that the justices will be "informed of" the proceedings. No witnesses testify

THROUGH THE COURT SYSTEM

First Stop: State Court
Almost all cases (about 95 percent) start in state courts. These courts go by various names, depending on the state in which they operate: circuit, district, municipal, county, or superior. The case is tried and decided by a judge, a panel of judges, or a jury.

The side that loses can then appeal to the next level.

First Stop: Federal Court
U.S. DISTRICT COURT—About 5 percent of cases begin their journey in federal court. Most of these cases concern federal laws, the U.S. Constitution, or disputes that involve two or more states. They are heard in one of the ninety-four U.S. district courts in the nation.

U.S. COURT OF INTERNATIONAL TRADE—Federal court cases involving international trade appear in the U.S. Court of International Trade.

U.S. CLAIMS COURT—The U.S. Claims Court hears federal cases that involve more than $10,000, Indian claims, and some disputes with government contractors.

The loser in federal court can appeal to the next level.

Appeals: State Cases
Forty states have appeals courts that hear cases that have come from the state courts. In states without an appeals court, the case goes directly to the state supreme court.

Appeals: Federal Cases
U.S. CIRCUIT COURT—Cases appealed from U.S. district courts go to U.S. circuit courts of appeals. There are twelve circuit courts that handle cases from throughout the

nation. Each district court and every state and territory are assigned to one of the twelve circuits. Appeals in a few state cases—those that deal with rights guaranteed by the U.S. Constitution—are also heard in this court.

U.S. COURT OF APPEALS—Cases appealed from the U.S. Court of International Trade and the U.S. Claims Court are heard by the U.S. Court of Appeals for the Federal Circuit. Among the cases heard in this court are those involving patents and minor claims against the federal government.

Further Appeals: State Supreme Court

Cases appealed from state appeals courts go to the highest courts in the state—usually called supreme court. In New York, the state's highest court is called the court of appeals. Most state cases do not go beyond this point.

Final Appeals: U.S. Supreme Court

The U.S. Supreme Court is the highest court in the country. Its decision on a case is the final word. The Court decides issues that can affect every person in the nation. It has decided cases on slavery, abortion, school segregation, and many other important issues.

The Court selects the cases it will hear—usually around one hundred each year. Four of the nine justices must vote to consider a case in order for it to be heard. Almost all cases have been appealed from the lower courts (either state or federal).

Most people seeking a decision from the Court submit a petition for *certiorari*. Certiorari means that the case will be moved from a lower court to a higher court for review. The Court receives about nine thousand of these requests annually. The petition outlines the case and gives reasons why the Court should review it.

In rare cases, for example *New York Times* v. *United States*, an issue must be decided immediately. When such a case is of national importance, the Court allows it to bypass the usual lower court system and hears the case directly.

To win a spot on the Court's docket, a case must fall within one of the following categories:

• Disputes between states and the federal government or between two or more states. The Court also reviews cases involving ambassadors, consuls, and foreign ministers.

• Appeals from state courts that have ruled on a federal question.

• Appeals from federal appeals courts (about two-thirds of all requests fall into this category).

before the Court; the justices must rely on the records of testimony at the lower court trial.

The U.S. Supreme Court rules on cases that will set standards of law for the nation. Judges in lower courts use Supreme Court decisions as guides when issuing their own rulings.

Usually the chief justice chooses cases he believes are important and submits the list to the associate justices during a private conference. Sometimes, associate justices also select cases they think should be considered. During the conference, the justices review the cases and decide which ones should be scheduled for a hearing. To be heard, a case must get the votes of at least four of the nine justices.

PETITIONING TO BE HEARD

On January 17, 1968, Dan Johnston filed a petition for *certiorari* with the U.S. Supreme Court. The students would now be the petitioners in the case. David Ellenhorn and Melvin L. Wulf, two lawyers working with the national ACLU, helped Johnston prepare the petition. They would also do much of the work on the brief filed later with the Court. In making their appeal for a hearing, the lawyers outlined the details of the case and argued that the school board's policy had violated the students' constitutional right to free speech. They cited the *Burnside* v. *Byars* opinion and noted the similarity between the two cases. The *Burnside* opinion favored the students while the *Tinker* decision supported the school board; they noted that the conflict could only be resolved by the Supreme Court. As in the lower courts, the petition pitted the students (with their fathers listed as "next friend") against the school district, the school board members, the superintendent, the five principals, the director of education, math teacher Richard Moberly, girls' adviser Vera Tarmann, and several other school officials.

The attorneys for the school district, referred to as the respondents, submitted their brief on February 12, 1968. Des Moines attorneys Herschel G. Langdon and David W. Belin joined Herrick and Lovrien in drafting the document. They argued that the students should not be given a hearing. It should be left to local officials to determine how schools were run, the brief contended. Des Moines school authorities took reasonable steps to maintain order when they banned the protest. Without the ban, the lawyers said, many more students probably would have worn armbands, and that could very well have caused a commotion in the schools.

Authorities should not have to wait for a major disturbance to occur before taking action, the lawyers argued. "Secondary school authorities are surely not obliged to let events take their course before adopting rules and regulations." The brief echoed Lovrien's warning to the Eighth Circuit that "the courts should not 'second guess' the administrators" as long as the rules they made were reasonable. School officials "have a right to exercise their own judgment and discretion in promulgating the rules, including those which in some degree limit the students' right of free speech and free expression," the lawyers concluded.

On March 4, the Supreme Court announced that it would hear the *Tinker* case.

Brief for the students

Both sides now focused on preparing briefs to win the support of the justices. The Court relies on the briefs to detail the facts of the case, bolster arguments by citing previous court decisions that relate to the issues under discussion, and offer clear reasons why their side should prevail. That is exactly what the lawyers in the *Tinker* case attempted to do.

The students' lawyers devoted almost a third of their thirty-three-page brief to a detailed account of the armband incident. Their main argument in the brief, submitted June 1, 1968, focused on the students' First Amendment rights. "The First Amendment," they wrote, "protects the rights of public school students to free speech in their schools and classrooms."

The decision by the students to wear the small strips of black cloth (one to two inches wide and eight to nine inches long) arose from the "religious, ethical and moral environment" in which they were raised, the brief noted.

In making their case, they relied heavily on the 1943 U.S. Supreme Court ruling in *West Virginia State Board of Education* v. *Barnette*. That decision upheld the right of two Jehovah's Witness students to refrain from saying the Pledge of Allegiance along with their classmates because their religion prohibited them from uttering an oath to anyone but God. The *Tinker* brief quoted from the *Barnette* majority opinion written by Justice Robert Jackson: "The Fourteenth Amendment, as now applied to the States, protects the citizen against the State itself and all of its creatures—Boards of Education not excepted. These have, of course, important, delicate, and highly discretionary functions, but none that they may not perform within the limits of the Bill of Rights."

The brief went on to quote Justice Jackson's warning that schools, in particular, must safeguard students' rights as part of their duty to teach good citizenship. That schools "are educating the young for citizenship is reason for scrupulous protection of Constitutional freedoms of the individual," Jackson wrote, "if we are not to strangle the free mind at its source and teach youth to discount important principles of our government as mere platitudes."

IN 1943, TWO JEHOVAH'S WITNESSES WON THE RIGHT NOT TO RECITE THE
PLEDGE OF ALLEGIANCE IN CLASS WHEN THEIR CASE WENT TO THE SUPREME
COURT. THEIR ARGUMENT WAS THAT THEIR RELIGION DID NOT PERMIT THEM
TO UTTER AN OATH TO ANYONE BUT GOD.

The Court, in the *Barnette* case, did not allow the school board to infringe on students' First Amendment rights even to promote national unity during World War II, the students' lawyers noted.

Among other cases cited in the brief, the lawyers included *In re Gault*, a case involving the rights of juveniles charged of a crime. The majority opinion, written by Justice Abe Fortas the year before the *Tinker* case was heard, reasserted the rights of children: "Neither the Fourteenth Amendment nor the Bill of Rights is for adults alone." While acknowledging that school officials must be able to control conduct that interferes with learning, the need for order did not give authorities the right to ban free speech. Nor could they ban speech ahead of time (an action known as "prior restraint") without any evidence that the activity would be disruptive, the brief contended. Describing the armband protest as "dignified, orderly, and peaceful," the brief noted that officials had no reason to believe the students' acts would be disruptive.

The lawyers objected to the circuit court judge's ruling that the school's policy was reasonable. But being "reasonable" was not a strong enough reason to allow officials to deprive students of their rights. Only when students' speech would result in "clear, present and immediate" danger should officials be allowed to step in and prevent them from expressing themselves, the lawyers maintained.

The brief also cited *Burnside* v. *Byars*, the Fifth Circuit case, and another recent U.S. Supreme Court case, *Brown* v. *Louisiana*. In both cases, youths expressed views peacefully and were punished by authorities. In *Brown*, black students quietly sat in a public library to protest segregation of black and white library patrons. Both the Fifth Circuit and the Supreme Court upheld the youths' right to free expression.

That other students might cause disruptions because they disagreed with the armbands was no reason to ban the protest. Those disturbing the peace should be disciplined, not the student protesters. The lawyers pointed out that such expressions of protest "should stimulate response. That is the function and purpose of free speech and the educational process."

Furthermore, the brief stated, the school district's policy unfairly targeted only the black armbands worn to protest the Vietnam War. Officials had allowed students to wear other political and religious symbols, including the Nazi's Iron Cross. The brief contended that by singling out this particular symbol, school officials "struck at the very core of what the First Amendment protects—the expression of views which may be unpalatable" to most people. With that, the lawyers asked the Court to rule in favor of the students.

In addition to the briefs, the Court received an eighty-four-page document that included the lower court testimony, a newspaper article on the case, a copy of the principals' policy, Ross Peterson's proposed article for the school newspaper, E. Raymond Peterson's memo, statements by Leonard Tinker, and other court documents.

SCHOOL DISTRICT'S BRIEF

The school district's attorneys submitted their thirty-nine-page brief to the Court on June 24, 1968. They made these arguments:

- the board's policy did not deprive students of their right to free speech;

- disturbances in schools should be treated differently from those in other public places, like streets or bus depots;

• the ban on armbands was "reasonably calcu-
lated" to uphold discipline in the schools.

Like the students' brief, the school district's document opened with a thorough description of the events
surrounding the armband protest. The lawyers began
their argument by quoting the district court judge: "[Des
Moines school officials] have the responsibility for maintaining a scholarly, disciplined atmosphere within the
classroom. These officials not only have a right, they have
an obligation to prevent anything which might be disruptive of such an atmosphere. Unless the actions of school
officials in this connection are unreasonable, the Courts
should not interfere." As previously noted, the judge
ruled that the Des Moines officials had acted reasonably
in banning the students' armbands.

The brief cited the Fifth Circuit Court's *Blackwell*
decision to bolster their case: "A valuable constitutional
right is involved *and decisions must be made on a case by
case basis.*" Furthermore, the lawyers included a line
quoted in the Blackwell case and in many other proceedings: "The constitutional guarantee of freedom of speech
'does not confer an absolute right to speak.'" Justice
Edward Sanford first used the words in a 1925 free-speech
case, *Gitlow* v. *People of New York*, which put certain
restrictions on speech that threatened the welfare of
others.

In the brief, the lawyers disputed the students' statements that they had decided for themselves to wear the
armbands to school. The student protest, the school district contended, was "a propaganda program" originated
by the leftist group Students for a Democratic Society and
adults involved in the peace movement. They questioned
whether the Reverend Tinker had used his children to
"infiltrate the school with his propaganda."

The brief repeated E. Raymond Peterson's testimony that school officials instituted the ban because they believed the protest would disrupt classes at the schools. It also gave a summary of Peterson's memo detailing the reasons for the policy.

Outside agitators and local people demonstrated at the January board meeting, according to the brief. "On several occasions it was a little bit touch-and-go as far as maintaining order," the lawyers added. Without the "prompt action by the school administration," the brief contended, the armband protest could well have spiraled out of control as reported at other demonstrations throughout the country. Based on John Tinker's statement that someone had told him of threats and punches thrown, the lawyers argued that the protest had indeed caused a disturbance.

The brief contended that protests in the streets may be tolerated to a greater extent than disturbances in public buildings such as libraries and schools. The attorneys quoted at length Justice Hugo Black's dissent in the *Brown* v. *Louisiana* case. They emphasized one particularly relevant statement: If states cannot enforce rules and regulations in libraries, Black said, "I suppose that inevitably the next step will be to paralyze the schools." The First Amendment, he added, "does not guarantee to any person the right to use someone else's property, even that owned by government and dedicated to other purposes, as a stage to express dissident ideas." Likewise, argued the brief's authors, the students' parents and the SDS should not be allowed to "infiltrate the schools" with their protests and disrupt "the scholarly discipline" required at schools.

The brief cited another case, *Cox* v. *New Hampshire*, to support its contention that the district's policy was constitutional. In the *Cox* case, the Court ruled against

Jehovah's Witnesses who had been convicted for conducting a parade without a permit. In determining that the state did not violate the religious group's rights, the Court noted that without public order "liberty itself would be lost in the excesses of unrestrained abuses."

The law in Iowa authorized school officials to adopt "reasonable rules and regulations governing the conduct of the pupils," the lawyers noted. They argued that the rule banning armbands was reasonable. Because the rule was reasonable, they concluded, the Court should accept the district's right to regulate the schools and not "substitute its judgment for the judgment of the directors of the school district."

The brief cited several other cases in which courts allowed schools to make rules that affected students in various ways. In one case, *Byrd* v. *Gary*, the South Carolina District Court upheld the expulsion of students who tried to organize a boycott to protest the food served in the school cafeteria.

In concluding their brief, the school district's lawyers tried to separate their case from *Barnette* and others like it. The students' armband protest, according to the brief, had "no religious significance whatever." Quoting yet another case, *Board of Directors of Independent School District of Waterloo* v. *Green*, the brief noted that the court's duty was "to uphold a school regulation unless it is clearly arbitrary and unreasonable." If, instead, the courts chose to step in and regulate the schools, it "would result in confusion detrimental to the management, progress and efficient operation of our public school system."

The brief made its final pitch: The school district's ban on armbands was a reasonable way to head off anticipated disruption in the schools; for that reason, the Court should uphold the rule.

AMICUS BRIEF

Courts allow people who have an interest in a case to file *amicus curiae* (meaning "friend of the court") briefs supporting either side of an issue. Only in rare instances does the Court allow such advocates to participate in oral arguments.

In the *Tinker* case, Charles Morgan Jr. and Roy Lucas made their case for the students in an *amicus* brief filed June 3. They represented the U.S. National Student Association, an organization comprised of more than 300 college and university student governments. The young lawyers would work together again on cases that led to the Supreme Court's ruling in *Roe* v. *Wade* that guaranteed a woman's right to an abortion.

In the *Tinker amicus* brief, the lawyers argued that allowing high school students more freedoms would help prepare them for college and provide the nation with citizens "better prepared to deal with the complexities of a modern changing society." Like Johnston, the *amicus* lawyers cited the *Barnette* and *In re Gault* decisions. They contended that under the Constitution, public school officials could not prevent students from silently expressing their views through symbols like armbands. Only after such action "imminently threatens orderly operation of the classroom or . . . school" could officials step in and stop such a silent protest, they said. The students' actions in the *Tinker* case, the brief noted, did not present a "clear and present danger" to justify suppressing free speech—as required by the *Barnette* ruling.

From the previous cases, the brief's authors concluded that "a state cannot relegate its young citizens to second-class status where rights of political expression are concerned." If the school board's ban was allowed to stand, the lawyers argued, student expression could be thwarted by rules imposed at the "whim or convenience" of school officials. Under such a system, they said, public schools would be converted "into quiet military academies."

The brief acknowledged that school officials have the power to stop activity that would "inevitably create major disorders in the classroom," such as neon signs or giant posters. But the *Tinker* students' behavior, the brief noted, caused no such disturbances and should be treated differently. And it contended that threats of violence by those who disagree should not prevent students from speaking freely. Otherwise, "the right to speak would then be narrowed to the meaningless right to agree."

With the briefs in, the Court scheduled oral arguments in the case for November 12, 1968. The lawyers would spend the next few months preparing once again to sway the justices to their cause.

four
BEFORE THE COURT

Lawyers appearing before the U.S. Supreme Court step into history. They become actors in a drama that will forever be imprinted in the nation's record books. Imagine the thrill of walking up the long marble staircase leading into the Supreme Court building on the way to argue a case. Towering above, sixteen massive ribbed columns support the front entrance. A group of marble sculptures under the peaked roof represent "Liberty Enthroned" guarded by "Order and Authority." Below the sculptures, the motto, "Equal Justice Under Law," proclaims the Court's mission. To the right of the steps, a statue of a man representing law greets those who pass; to the left, the stone figure of a seated woman represents justice.

Sculpted bronze doors lead into the Great Hall, where the busts of past Supreme Court chief justices gaze down on passersby. A nervous lawyer might understandably pause before opening the heavy oak doors into the Court chambers at the east end of the hall. There, too, the room reflects the dignified grandeur of the Court.

Twenty-four columns of Italian marble support the high ceiling. The justices' raised mahogany bench gleams under the overhead lights. In 1965, when lawyers argued the *Tinker* case, the bench formed a straight line behind which the nine justices sat. As part of a renovation project in 1972, the bench was curved so that justices could see and hear each other better during oral arguments.

Standing on red carpet, the lawyers anxiously view the red velvet curtains through which the justices will emerge. At the marshal's call, the nine justices file into the room, led by the chief justice. The chief justice sits in the center, with the most senior associate justice to the right, the second most senior justice to the left, and so on, alternating right and left by seniority. At the chief justice's invitation, the petitioner's lawyer walks to the podium and begins his or her argument. Each lawyer has thirty minutes to make his or her case. A time clock hangs prominently above the bench to remind lawyers of the passing time. On the lectern two lights, one white and one red, serve as further reminders of the time limit. The white light warns the lawyer that he or she has only five more minutes to conclude arguments. When the red light goes on, the argument is over unless the justices themselves ask the lawyer to continue.

controversy and change

Snow mixed with rain clogged the streets and snarled traffic in Washington, D.C., on November 12, 1968, the day scheduled for the *Tinker* arguments before the U.S. Supreme Court. A blizzard delayed the flight of John Tinker, by now a student at the University of Iowa, and prevented him from reaching the Court in time for the arguments in the case that bore his name. His sister, Mary Beth, his parents, and other siblings attended, as did Christopher Eckhardt and his parents.

Much had happened since the time, almost three years earlier, when the students had first decided to don black armbands to mourn the dead in Vietnam and support a truce proposed by Senator Robert F. Kennedy. During the excruciatingly slow odyssey from court to court, Christopher Eckhardt and John Tinker graduated from high school and went on to college. Mary Beth and her parents moved to St. Louis, Missouri, where she was a junior at University City High School. Christopher's parents relocated to Canada, where William Eckhardt worked for the Canadian Peace Research Institute.

During those three years, too, a Palestinian Arab by the name of Sirhan Sirhan, angered by Senator Robert Kennedy's support of Israel, had shot and killed him as he walked through a hotel food service pantry while campaigning for president.

In Vietnam, the war raged on. In 1965, an average of 172 U.S. soldiers died in the war each month. Two years later, the monthly average of American soldiers killed rose to 770. At the end of 1968, 537,000 U.S. forces were serving in Vietnam.

During the Vietnamese Tet holiday in January 1968, North Vietnamese and Viet Cong forces seized control of several cities in the south. American soldiers eventually drove them back in a major defeat of the communists. But the initial success of the North disheartened Americans back home. Many observers later believed the Tet Offensive was the turning point of the war. Frustrated citizens aimed their criticism at President Lyndon B. Johnson for what they regarded as his mishandling of the war. A defeated Johnson—the president who had once promised to bring peace to Vietnam and then ordered massive air raids against the enemy—announced in March 1968 that he would not run for reelection. Just days before the Court heard oral arguments in the *Tinker* case, the voters elected Richard M. Nixon as the nation's thirty-seventh president. Like Johnson, he had campaigned on a pledge of bringing the war to an end.

Protests against the war became more prevalent and more impassioned. Brothers Daniel and Philip Berrigan and others were arrested countless times as they occupied military bases and threw blood on the walls to protest the war. Student groups staged sit-ins, and more radical groups sponsored other acts of civil disobedience on college campuses. The war became less and less popular among U.S. citizens. Massive antiwar demonstrations in Washington, D.C., New York City, and elsewhere attracted thousands of middle-class Americans. In August 1965, 61 percent of the American public supported the United States' role in the Vietnam War, according to polls taken at the time. After the Tet Offensive, the country remained bitterly divided on the issue, but support for the war began to slip. By early 1968, 49 percent of Americans told pollsters that they thought the war was "a mistake." Only 26 percent approved of the way Johnson had conducted the war.

ROBED JUSTICES

While the outside world continued the loud and persistent debate over the war, inside the courtroom the participants in the armband case waited nervously for the justices to appear. "Oyez, oyez, oyez!" the marshal called, an ancient term meaning "hear ye." Everyone in the courtroom stood. The nine black-robed justices entered and sat in the black leather chairs facing the room.

These men, who would decide the students' case, came from diverse backgrounds and held a wide range of views. Although most could be grouped in conservative or liberal camps, no one could predict with absolute accuracy how each might vote on a particular case. More than once, a so-called liberal justice had cast his vote on the conservative side of things and vice versa.

Chief Justice Earl Warren sat in the center of the nine justices. He had been appointed to the Court in 1953. As a district attorney and attorney general of California,

PRESIDENT LYNDON B. JOHNSON DECIDED NOT TO RUN FOR REELECTION IN 1968—MOST PEOPLE BELIEVE THAT HIS STEPPING UP OF THE WAR IN VIETNAM RESULTED IN HIS STEPPING DOWN FROM HIGH OFFICE.

RICHARD M. NIXON WAS ELECTED PRESIDENT IN 1968. HE CAMPAIGNED ON A PLEDGE TO END THE WAR IN VIETNAM, BUT U.S. FORCES DID NOT WITHDRAW UNTIL WELL INTO HIS SECOND TERM.

Warren earned a reputation as a conservative and a crime fighter. A former governor of California, Warren was nominated by President Dwight D. Eisenhower, who later called the nomination "the biggest damn-fool mistake I ever made." Eisenhower's change of heart derived from a string of liberal landmark decisions delivered under Warren's leadership. The decisions guaranteed civil liberties to a wide range of citizens, including black school children's right to equal education, the right to counsel for indigent defendants, and the right to privacy for married couples.

To Warren's right sat Hugo L. Black, the justice who had served the longest on the Court. Appointed to the Court in 1937, Black had gained fame while a public prosecutor in Alabama for his investigation of police brutality while questioning suspects. He served as a U.S. senator before being nominated to the Court by President Franklin D. Roosevelt. Perhaps of all the justices, Black had taken the strongest stand for First Amendment rights in past decisions.

U.S. CHIEF JUSTICE EARL WARREN, THOUGH APPOINTED BY A REPUBLICAN PRESIDENT, PROVED TO BE THE MOST LIBERAL CHIEF JUSTICE THE SUPREME COURT HAS SEEN. HE PRESIDED OVER THE *TINKER* CASE.

William O. Douglas, the second most senior justice, sat to the left of Warren. Douglas taught at Columbia and Yale Law Schools and served as chair of the U.S. Securities and Exchange Commission before his appointment to the Court in 1939. He, too, was nominated by Roosevelt. Like Black, he was a firm believer in preserving First Amendment rights and other civil liberties.

Beside Black sat John Marshall Harlan, nominated to the Court in 1955 by Eisenhower. He had served as assistant U.S. attorney, special assistant to the attorney general of New York, and on the U.S. Court of Appeals. He was named for his grandfather, Supreme Court Justice John Marshall Harlan, who served on the Court from 1877 to 1911. Known as the court's conservative conscience, Harlan often defended states' rights. But he also had voted for individual rights in several landmark cases, including the *Brown* v. *Board of Education II* case that enforced the 1954 *Brown* v. *Board of Education* decision and led to desegregation in the schools.

On Harlan's right was Potter Stewart. He had worked briefly as a Wall Street lawyer and had served on the Sixth Circuit Court of Appeals before joining the Court. An Eisenhower nominee, he was appointed to the Court in 1959. Raised in a conservative Republican family, Stewart often found himself following a middle course on the Court. He frequently sided with his liberal colleagues on First Amendment cases and with more conservative brethren on other issues.

Abe Fortas, a Lyndon B. Johnson nominee appointed in 1965, sat on the end next to Stewart. He had taken stands for civil liberties before. A brilliant lawyer, Fortas had argued successfully in the 1963 landmark case, *Gideon* v. *Wainwright*, to guarantee the right to an attorney for all defendants. The year before the *Tinker* arguments, he had written the Court's landmark decision for *In re Gault* that

JUSTICE WILLIAM O. DOUGLAS WAS KNOWN AS A STAUNCH DEFENDER OF
FIRST AMENDMENT RIGHTS AND CIVIL LIBERTIES.

granted civil rights to juveniles involved in court cases. Even so, Fortas had voted against granting the *Tinker* case a hearing during the private session the justices held to discuss upcoming cases. At the time of the arguments, no one other than the justices themselves and their aides knew who had voted for or against hearing the *Tinker* case. Fortas later revealed that he was reluctant to interfere in school discipline.

On the other side of the bench, to the left of Douglas, sat William Joseph Brennan Jr., an Eisenhower nominee appointed to the Court in 1956. Brennan had served as a New Jersey Superior Court judge and as an associate judge on the state supreme court before being named to the High Court. One of the most liberal justices, he championed the rights of the individual. Brennan's liberal votes and leadership led Eisenhower to rue yet another of his nominations to the Court.

Byron R. White, the only appointee of President John F. Kennedy on the Court, sat next to Brennan. A professional football player in his youth, White had served as deputy U.S. attorney general in Kennedy's administration before his appointment in 1962. Like Stewart, White often played a centrist role on the Court. Much more conservative than Kennedy had been on many civil liberty issues, White prided himself on being an independent thinker.

Thurgood Marshall, the Court's newest member and the only African American, sat on the end next to White. Nominated by President Lyndon B. Johnson, Marshall had argued many civil rights cases before the Court as an attorney for the National Association for the Advancement of Colored People before joining the bench in 1967. He led the defense in the school segregation cases. Considered a member of the liberal branch of the Court, Marshall supported racial equality and individual rights.

The justices peered down from the elevated bench as the Court waded through a mountain of cases. Dan Johnston, lawyer for the Des Moines students, and Allan A. Herrick, representing the school board, sat anxiously awaiting their turn. The morning began with Associate Justice Abe Fortas's reading of the Court's decision in another First Amendment school case, *Epperson* v. *Arkansas*. In that case, a unanimous Court ruled in favor of teachers who had sought the right to teach Darwin's theory of evolution in public schools. An Arkansas law banned public school teachers and professors in state-supported universities from teaching the theory. The justices based their decision on the Fourteenth and First Amendments. But unlike the *Tinker* case, which relied on the First Amendment's guarantee of free speech, the *Epperson* decision was based on the amendment's ban against establishment of religion by the government.

JOHNSTON ARGUES HIS CASE

While the lawyers and the observers in the *Tinker* case waited impatiently, the Court delivered opinions in seven cases and tended to a long list of routine matters. Proceedings stretched into midafternoon. Finally, after a lunch break and oral arguments in two other cases, Chief Justice Earl Warren announced case number 21, *John F. and Mary Beth Tinker* v. *Des Moines Independent Community School District*. Lawyer Dan Johnston got to his feet as Chief Justice Warren called his name.

At first, Johnston compared his case to *Epperson* as both involving individual rights in the schools. Justice Fortas, however, quickly made it clear that he thought the cases addressed two entirely different topics: free speech in *Tinker* and freedom of religion in *Epperson*.

For the next five or six minutes, Johnston described in detail the events leading up to the case. He told the Court of the experiences of Christopher Eckhardt and Mary Beth Tinker on the day they wore armbands to school. The lawyer had just begun detailing John Tinker's story on the following day when Justice Byron White asked the first question.

Justice White wanted to know what would have happened if one of the protesting students had delivered the antiwar message aloud instead of silently wearing an armband. "In that case, your honor, we would not be here," Johnston replied.

The justice pressed him with a series of questions on whether the armband distracted students' attention from classroom work. "[The armband] wouldn't cause a commotion, but don't you think that it would cause some people to direct their attention to the armband and the Vietnam war and think about that rather than what they were . . . supposed to be thinking about in the classroom?" Justice White asked.

None of the teachers who testified in the lower courts about the case had complained that the armbands were disruptive, Johnston said. He acknowledged that students' attention might be diverted for a "few moments." But, he noted, school officials allowed all kinds of things that distracted students. Rather than being distracting, Johnston argued, the armbands contributed to the school's "total atmosphere," presumably by presenting students with an issue to be explored.

Justice Thurgood Marshall ended Justice White's probing questions and threw Johnston a lifeline. In response to Marshall's questioning, Johnston revealed that the school's policy was not limited to the classroom. It barred students from wearing armbands anywhere in the building.

Johnston contended that the school's policy was far too broad to "stand the test of freedom of expression

PEACE DEMONSTRATIONS WERE NOT ALWAYS PEACEFUL. HERE, A PEACE DEMONSTRATOR IS KNOCKED TO THE GROUND AS HE TRIES TO BREAK THROUGH POLICE LINES IN FRONT OF THE PENTAGON.

under the First Amendment." But he argued that even if the policy banned armbands only in the classroom, it still should not be allowed. Students were merely expressing their opinion—a freedom guaranteed by the First Amendment. The school had no grounds to infringe on the students' rights because their actions caused no harm and no disruption.

What if the students' protest started fist fights among other students, Chief Justice Warren wanted to know. Couldn't the principal ban the armbands in that case?

Johnston disagreed. Instead of taking away First Amendment rights, he said, the school should discipline the troublemakers. People in schools should have the same right to free speech as anyone else, he argued. "There should not be any special rule for freedom of expression cases for schools," he told the chief justice.

To bolster his argument, Johnston relied on a 1949 U.S. Supreme Court case, *Terminiello* v. *Chicago*. In that case, Father Arthur Terminiello was arrested and convicted for inciting a riot after his fiery speech caused disturbances among the angry crowd. The U.S. Supreme Court ultimately ruled that the Constitution protected Terminiello's freedom of speech—even though the priest's speech led to disturbances. Speech could be stopped, the Court said, only when it was "likely to produce a clear and present danger of a serious substantive evil that rises far above public inconvenience, annoyance, or unrest." In his opinion for the Court, Justice William Douglas went so far as to say that such disturbances benefited the nation: "A function of free speech under our system is to invite dispute. It may indeed best serve its high purpose when it induces a condition of unrest, creates dissatisfaction with conditions as they are, or even stirs people to anger."

Johnston acknowledged that school officials would be justified in disciplining students whose actions significantly interfered with the teacher's lesson. He referred to the *Burnside* v. *Byars* case outlined in his brief. The Fifth

Circuit Court sided with students who wore political buttons in that case because their actions did not "materially and substantially interfere with" school discipline. The same reasoning should apply in the armband case, Johnston noted. "It was the principle of the demonstration, the idea of expressing political beliefs that [school officials] were opposed to in this context and the students were suspended for violating that policy and not suspended for causing any disruption in the classroom," he told the Court.

The Court should focus not on the behavior of the students, Johnston suggested, but on that of school officials. Should the authorities be allowed, he asked, to "punish freedom of expression" when students had done nothing to harm public interest?

Justice Stewart wondered why the case wasn't moot. The Court will not hear a case based solely on an abstract question. If the plaintiffs are no longer affected by the controversy or the situation has been resolved, the case may be considered moot, or abstract, and no longer under consideration by the Court. In the armband case, the students were back in school and were not being punished for their actions.

According to Johnston, the students continued to be affected by the school policy because they still wanted to wear armbands "to express their opposition to the war in Vietnam."

And if the war were to end before the Court decided the case? asked Justice John Harlan.

Even if the Vietnam War ended that day, Johnston noted, the students still had suffered from the school officials' actions. They missed classes during the time they were suspended, and they were not allowed to express their beliefs. The case, the young lawyer said, offered an excellent opportunity for the Court to lay down guidelines for future suits involving students' rights to free expression.

Justice Harlan feared such a judgment would mire the Court "pretty deep in the trenches" of routine school decisions. But Johnston noted that the Court had already ruled on a number of school cases, including the *Epperson* case decided that morning. Whatever "delicate functions" school boards must undertake, the lawyer said, they still must operate under the requirements of the First Amendment.

Responding to a question by Justice Abe Fortas, Johnston said that wearing outrageous clothes probably did not qualify as free expression and would not be protected under the First Amendment. Views expressed by kindergarten students, however, should be protected, he noted. Again he stated his opinion that there should not be "a special rule" for schools regarding First Amendment rights. With a few minutes to spare, Johnston ended his argument, reserving the remaining time until the end of the session.

SCHOOL DISTRICT Takes a Turn

Chief Justice Warren then turned the proceedings over to Allan Herrick, attorney for the school board. Herrick began by making three points:

> 1. School authorities should not have to wait until mayhem breaks out before banning certain student activity.
>
> 2. The Court should leave discipline up to school officials and not review "every decision of every school district made in good faith."
>
> 3. Disturbances in schools should be judged differently from those on public streets.

He noted that the Court had imposed restrictions on freedom of speech in the past. In making his case, he cited the recent decision in *Adderley* v. *Florida*. The case involved more than one hundred students at Florida Agricultural & Mechanical University who were arrested when they blocked the local jail driveway while protesting the arrest of other students. The Court ruled in the state's favor. According to the decision, the First Amendment's guarantee of free speech did not prevent the state from controlling the protesters and protecting its property. Justice Black delivered the opinion in the 1966 case, concluding: "The United States Constitution does not forbid a State to control the use of its own property for its own lawful nondiscriminatory purpose."

But Justice Marshall quickly dispelled any comparisons between the two cases. He noted that the armband case involved only seven students, a far cry from the hundred or more in *Adderley*. "Seven out of eighteen thousand and the school board was afraid that seven students wearing armbands would disrupt eighteen thousand," Marshall commented sardonically.

The embattled lawyer defended the school board's right to decide "in good faith" what actions they believed needed to be taken to prevent disturbances at the schools.

Justice Marshall continued to push Herrick for evidence that the wearing of the armbands disrupted the schools. "The school system was aroused? Where is that in the record?" he asked.

Herrick answered by reiterating the events that led up to the school's policy. He noted that controversy over the Vietnam War had become heated. When the school board held a hearing to vote on the armband policy that school officials had adopted, some 200 people showed up. "It is against this background that the Court must review the reasonableness of the regulation," Herrick said.

Chief Justice Warren interjected with a question of his own. Communities throughout the nation, he noted, had debated the issues "argumentatively and vociferously" during the 1968 presidential race. "Do you think then that [the controversy over the war] is a sufficient backdrop for stopping First Amendment rights in all of these communities?"

Herrick tried to put the school board's action in perspective. He noted that free discussion in the classroom "is always permitted." But, he added, courts needed to weigh the students' right to free expression against the schools' obligation to maintain "a scholarly, disciplined atmosphere" in the classroom. School officials, he said, not only had a right but a duty to prevent actions that would disrupt the learning environment.

"Sometimes an ounce of prevention is a lot better than a pound of cure and I think subsequent history of such activities bear out the judgment of the school officials and their discretion," Herrick said.

Chief Justice Warren wondered how far school officials could take that premise. Could they, for instance, ban all discussion of political matters?

No, Herrick quickly replied. But they could, he argued, determine when and where the discussion would take place.

Throughout his argument, Herrick contended that the situation was "inflammatory" and "explosive." Both Chief Justice Warren and Justice Marshall pressed him on the point. "What evidence is there of explosiveness in the community?" Chief Justice Warren asked. After reading John Tinker's testimony that no threats were made against him, Herrick found a passage that referred to "some accounts of . . . physical violence" against "some students."

If there had been physical violence, Justice Marshall

challenged, wouldn't school officials have known about it? And, he continued, wouldn't they have used it in their court statements to prove their point?

Herrick had to admit that was a reasonable assumption. Nonetheless, he clung to his argument that controversy over the Vietnam War created an "explosive situation." A former student at the school had been killed in Vietnam, he noted, and school officials feared the armband demonstration might outrage some of his friends who still attended school in Des Moines.

"Do we have a city in this country that hasn't had someone killed in Vietnam?" Marshall asked.

No, Herrick acknowledged. But not every city had students who wore armbands to school, he added.

The lawyer got a welcome helping hand from Justice Black. The justice restated Herrick's case for him: "What you claim is that you have the right to run your school [for] the teaching of geometry, history, mathematics, grammar, and the things that people want to teach and that the federal constitution doesn't step in and tell you that you've got to let anybody discuss any subject symbolically or otherwise as they see fit."

Justice Black further guided Herrick to say that freedom of expression should not interfere with teaching. "I believe the schools are there to give these children an education," he said under Black's prompting. "I feel that anything that threatens that type of scholarly atmosphere in the classroom ought to be prohibited."

Again, Chief Justice Warren noted that students wearing the armbands caused no disruption. Justice White, however, pointed out that the class discussed the protest during mathematics class instead of studying that topic.

At that point, Justice Stewart asked about the claim that the schools had allowed other students to wear political buttons and Iron Crosses, the symbol of the Nazi party. Herrick confirmed that that was so.

Discussion then turned to yet another previous case. Justice Fortas asked Herrick to comment on the Court's decision in *Meyer* v. *Nebraska*. The case, decided in 1923, concerned a Nebraska law that made it illegal to teach German in schools in the state. The Court struck down the law, saying it violated the liberty of both teachers and parents guaranteed under the Fourteenth Amendment. Did that ruling, Justice Fortas asked, establish the right of the Court to overrule school boards when their actions are so unreasonable that they violate the Constitution?

Herrick restated his belief that the Court should consider each case separately. It would be very difficult, he said, for the Court to try to regulate every situation a school faced. Justice Fortas agreed that the Court would have a hard time reviewing every action of a school board and deciding whether it was reasonable.

"I think some things have got to be left to the judgment of the administrators," Herrick said.

The podium light turned red. His time ended, Herrick sat down.

FINAL WORDS

Dan Johnston used his few remaining minutes to emphasize that the Des Moines school officials had singled out this one political emblem to ban. The system, he said, had never stopped students from wearing political emblems other than the armbands. Johnston also disputed Herrick's contention that the situation at the schools was explosive. "I don't believe that the record supports that," he told the Court.

Under Justice Black's questioning, the students' lawyer agreed that the law of Iowa granted the school board the power to bar political discussion during school class time.

But, he said, that was not what the Des Moines board did. "They've banned only the discussion in one specific instance," he told the Court.

The policy should be ruled invalid, Johnston argued, not because it was unreasonable (as in the *Meyer* case), but because school officials did not prove that the armbands would create a disturbance so serious that it justified depriving students of their First Amendment right to freedom of expression.

The argument did not satisfy Justice Black. The state had an interest, he told Johnston, in trying to protect the right of school officials and teachers to run the schools as they saw fit. "Which do you think has the most . . . control in the schools . . . the pupils or the authorities that are running the schools?" Black asked.

The school officials, Johnston swiftly responded. But, he concluded, they must operate within the provisions of the Constitution that has granted them authority. "The whole nub of our case," he said, "[is] that they have exceeded their powers under [the Constitution]."

With that, Johnston ended his argument, and the Court adjourned.

FIVE
THE DECISION

AFTER LISTENING TO THE ORAL ARGUMENTS in the *Tinker* case, Christopher Eckhardt felt certain the Supreme Court would vote in the students' favor. "When I heard Justice Thurgood Marshall ask the question— 'Seven out of 18,000, and the school board was afraid that seven students wearing armbands would disrupt 18,000. Am I correct?'—then I was confident we would prevail," Eckhardt said during an interview marking the thirtieth anniversary of the decision.

Dan Johnston, attorney for the students in the *Tinker* case, held a similar optimistic view of the proceedings. According to John W. Johnson, author of a book on the case, *The Struggle for Student Rights*, Johnston believed that the students had a strong case and that the Court would rule in their favor.

BEHIND CLOSED DOORS
Once lawyers have argued a case before the U.S. Supreme Court, the justices hold a conference to discuss the issues raised in Court and in the briefs. Held behind closed doors, the meeting is attended only by the members of the Court. The chief justice gives his views, then each associate justice follows, beginning with the member who has served on the Court the longest and ending with the most junior member. After the review, the justices vote on the case.

On November 15, 1968, the justices held their conference on the *Tinker* case. During the discussions, Justice Hugo Black made it clear he favored the school board's argument. According to notes taken by fellow justices (and cited in John Johnson's book), Black lectured on "children being allowed to run riot" and the country "going to ruin." One other justice, John Marshall Harlan, sided with the school board. The other seven justices, including Chief Justice Earl Warren, supported the students in their suit.

Supreme Court justices are appointed to their post for life. Because of their life appointment, justices are not as vulnerable to the political pressures of elected officials. That does not mean, however, that they remain untouched by politics or by public opinion. The justices made their decision on the *Tinker* case in the midst of growing unrest among college students and faculty members. Justice Black was not merely posing a rhetorical question when he asked Dan Johnston during oral arguments who should control the schools. The eighty-two-year-old justice viewed the issue as one that could break down discipline in the schools and allow unruly students to run the show, as they seemed to be doing on many college campuses. That may help explain why the justice best known for his adamant support of First Amendment rights did not support the same rights for students.

Justice Black, however, failed to sway his colleagues. Seven justices remained firm in their decision to strike down the school board's ban on armbands.

If the chief justice sides with the majority, he selects who will write the opinion for the Court. The associate justice with the longest service on the Court among those who have voted for the majority chooses the author of the opinion if the chief justice votes with the minority. In this case, Chief Justice Warren chose Justice Abe Fortas to

This was the composition of the U.S. Supreme Court when the *Tinker* case was decided. Seated, from left: John Marshall Harlan, Hugo L. Black, Chief Justice Earl Warren, William O. Douglas, and William J. Brennan. Standing, from left: Abe Fortas, Potter Stewart, Byron White, and Thurgood Marshall.

THE *Tinker* DECISION WAS THE LAST SUPREME COURT CASE THAT ABE FORTAS WOULD WRITE DURING HIS SHORT, CONTROVERSIAL TENURE AS PRESIDENT LYNDON JOHNSON'S COURT APPOINTEE.

write the Court's decision. Fortas, who had been on the Court for only three years, had been the author of the *In re Gault* decision the year before.

The Court that decided the *Tinker* case may have seemed far removed from the political machinations going on in Congress. During the mid-1960s, the nation's elected officials engaged in bitter debate over the Vietnam War and President Lyndon B. Johnson's Great Society, an ambitious program that featured civil rights for African Americans, Medicare and Medicaid, and the so-called War on Poverty. Despite its seemingly exalted position, the *Tinker* Court was embroiled in the political warfare of the time. Chief Justice Earl Warren had announced earlier in the year that he wanted to retire. In June 1968 President Johnson had nominated his friend, Associate Justice Abe Fortas, as Warren's successor. But Johnson's enemies in Congress used the nomination to get back at the president's policies. They raised ethical questions about Fortas's business dealings, forcing Johnson to withdraw the associate justice's name. Attacks on the justice's ethics continued during the time the Court was considering the *Tinker* case. Fortas would resign under pressure the following May. The *Tinker* case would be the last decision he would write for the Court.

In writing an opinion, a justice often relies on past rulings to explain the reasoning behind the decision. Only rarely does a majority opinion overturn a ruling made by a previous Court. After the opinion has been drafted, the justices meet again for a second conference. Other justices may write their own opinions, either supporting the majority vote (a concurrence) or opposing it (a dissent). Sometimes, a well-worded dissent can persuade justices to change their vote. If that happens, a dissent may become the majority opinion. Justices may also ask for revisions in the majority opinion or require a major rewrite. Once they have agreed on a final draft, the Court delivers the decision and it becomes the law of the land.

students prevail

On February 24, 1969, Justice Abe Fortas read the Court's decision in the *Tinker* case. After a brief summary of the case, he restated the findings of the appeals court: Wearing the armbands was an act of expression protected under the First Amendment's free speech clause; the act caused no disruption; and students and teachers are entitled to First Amendment rights even under the special circumstances required to run a school. The Court, in a 7 to 2 decision, had ruled in the students' favor.

"It can hardly be argued that either students or teachers shed their constitutional rights to freedom of speech or expression at the schoolhouse gate," Justice Fortas said. The words would echo through the Court's marble halls in the years to come, as lawyers, judges, journalists, and others repeated them countless times to bolster new students' rights cases.

That conclusion—that students and teachers have rights, too—had been supported by the Court in decisions handed down for the past half century, Fortas continued. At the end of a long list of related decisions upholding that view, Justice Fortas quoted a passage from Justice Jackson's opinion in *West Virginia* v. *Barnette*, the same section the students' lawyers had cited in their brief:

> [Boards of education] have, of course, important, delicate, and highly discretionary functions, but none that they may not perform within the limits of the Bill of Rights. That they are educating the young for citizenship is reason for scrupulous protection of Constitutional freedoms of the individual, if we are not to strangle the free mind at its source and teach youth

to discount important principles of our government as mere platitudes.

The justice stressed the importance of allowing states and local school boards to run their own schools. But such authority, he noted, had to be "consistent with fundamental constitutional safeguards." In the *Tinker* case, he said, the students' free speech rights and the school officials' rules collided. The case did not revolve around clothing, disruptive acts, or group protests—which the Court had already left in the hands of local officials in previous cases. The issue at stake in the *Tinker* case, Justice Fortas pointed out, involved "direct, primary First Amendment rights akin to 'pure speech.'"

The First Amendment protected the students' symbolic speech—wearing armbands to school—just as much as their right to discuss their views on the Vietnam War, Fortas noted. "Our Constitution does not permit officials of the State to deny their form of expression."

There was no evidence that the students' acts disrupted the school or interfered with other students. School officials had argued in the lower courts and in their brief that they feared the armband demonstration would disrupt class work and interfere with school discipline. The district court agreed and ruled that the school board had acted reasonably when it banned the protest based on that fear. But Justice Fortas and the majority of the Court disagreed. The board's fear alone, without any evidence of a disturbance, was not enough to justify suppressing the students' right to free speech, according to Fortas. "In our system," he wrote, "undifferentiated fear or apprehension of disturbance is not enough to overcome the right to freedom of expression."

Inevitably, disagreements may arise and some people may be fearful when others express views that differ from those of the majority, Fortas continued. That is a risk people in a free society must take if they are to preserve their freedom. Such openness—what Justice Fortas termed "hazardous freedom"—is "the basis of our national strength and of the independence and vigor of Americans."

Fortas also noted that the school officials in the *Tinker* case allowed students to wear other types of symbols, including the Nazis' Iron Cross. The Constitution, the justice said, did not allow authorities to single out one symbol—the black armbands—because they did not agree with the sentiment they represented—opposition to the Vietnam conflict.

He stated again the principles that lay at the heart of the majority opinion. Students remain "persons" in school as well as outside its bounds. They have basic rights, among them the freedom to express their views. Authorities cannot run schools as "enclaves of totalitarianism." Under the Constitution, these officials must not suppress students' views merely because they disagree with them.

In making his point, Justice Fortas quoted Justice Brennan's majority opinion in *Keyishan* v. *Board of Regents*, another First Amendment case decided by the Court two years earlier:

> *The vigilant protection of constitutional freedoms is nowhere more vital than in the community of American schools. The classroom is peculiarly the "marketplace of ideas." The Nation's future depends upon leaders trained through wide exposure to that robust exchange of ideas which discovers truth "out of a multitude of tongues, [rather] than through any kind of authoritative selection."*

The majority opinion did not prohibit school officials from taking action to prevent student speech or actions that disrupted the school. Any conduct that "materially disrupt[ed] classwork," that resulted in "substantial disorder," or that interfered with the rights of others did not fall under the First Amendment protections, according to Justice Fortas. The Constitution permitted officials to make "reasonable regulation[s]" to control speech "in carefully restricted circumstances." But the rules, he noted, had to be based on "something more than a mere desire to avoid the discomfort and unpleasantness that always accompany an unpopular viewpoint."

Free speech that is limited to "a telephone booth . . . a pamphlet . . . or to supervised and ordained discussion in a school classroom" is not really free, Justice Fortas said. If officials had prohibited students from speaking against the Vietnam conflict anywhere on school grounds, he said, it would be "obvious" that such a rule was unconstitutional. Likewise, he concluded, the students' silent "witness of the armbands" fell under the same category, and school officials had no power, under the Constitution, to ban it.

The opinion reversed the appeals court decision and sent the case back to the lower courts to determine what compensation was due the students.

Two justices, Stewart and White, submitted short, separate concurring opinions. In his statement, Stewart agreed with the ultimate decision of the Court, but he said he believed children did not have the same rights as adults. Minors, "like someone in a captive audience," cannot make all life's choices for themselves and therefore do not fall under the full range of guarantees promised by the First Amendment.

White, too, agreed with the majority in the overall decision. He objected, however, to parts of the opinion in the *Burnside* v. *Byars* case, cited by the plaintiffs and by Justice Fortas, that defined free speech. White also noted the difference between free speech and acts that expressed views but that interfered with others.

A STINGING DISSENT

Justice Harlan filed a brief dissent that, like the concurring opinions, was less than 200 words long. He acknowledged that school officials could not completely ignore the rights of students. But, he contended, officials needed to have "the widest authority" in maintaining discipline and order at the schools. Harlan disagreed with the majority because, he said, the students had not shown that school officials ordered the ban for any reason other than "legitimate school concerns."

In a dissent as lengthy as the majority opinion, Justice Black stated his strong objections to the Court's decision. The ruling, he said, signaled the beginning of "an entirely new era" in which the Supreme Court took over the duties of public officials elected to run the schools. His forceful arguments backed the right of elected officials—not courts—to decide whether rules were reasonable or not.

In his bitter, sometimes sarcastic, opinion, Justice Black took the majority justices to task for what he viewed as turning over control of the schools to students. Among his doomsday predictions was the view that some students would take the ruling as permission to "defy their teachers on practically all orders."

The justice disagreed with the majority's contention that the armband protest did not disrupt the work of the school. "I think the record overwhelmingly shows that the armbands did exactly what the elected school officials and principals foresaw they would, that is, took the students' minds off their classwork and diverted them to thoughts about the highly emotional subject of the Vietnam war."

The First Amendment advocate gave little credence

JUSTICE JOHN H. HARLAN STRONGLY DISSENTED FROM THE COURT'S DECISION IN *TINKER.*

to the students' claim that the school had suppressed their right to free speech. Instead, he attacked the notion that students could deliberately refuse to obey school officials' orders. "If the time has come when pupils of state-supported schools, kindergartens, grammar schools, or high schools, can defy and flout orders of school officials to keep their minds on their own schoolwork," he warned, "it is the beginning of a new revolutionary era of permissiveness in this country fostered by the judiciary."

He predicted the next step would be for students to push for the vote and for representation on school boards themselves.

Justice Black also objected to the Court's reliance on the reasonable test when judging whether the school board's rules violated the Constitution's due process requirement. Such a test, he contended, had long been out of favor. Resurrecting the test, he said, wrongfully gave judges the "power to strike down any law they [did] not like."

Justice Fortas's contention that students and teachers did not "shed their constitutional rights . . . at the school-house gate" met with similar objections from Justice Black. "The truth is that a teacher of kindergarten, grammar school, or high school pupils no more carries into a school with him a complete right to freedom of speech and expression than an anti-Catholic or anti-Semite carries with him a complete freedom of speech and religion into a Catholic church or Jewish synagogue," Black noted.

Although Black had long been a champion of First Amendment guarantees of free speech and freedom of the press, he did not support the same sweeping protections for disruptive symbolic speech and conduct. "It is a myth to say that any person has a constitutional right to say what he pleases, where he pleases, and when he pleases," he

JUSTICE HUGO BLACK, THOUGH LONG A CHAMPION OF FIRST AMENDMENT
RIGHTS OF FREE SPEECH, FELT THAT LIMITS SHOULD APPLY WHEN THAT
SPEECH WAS DISRUPTIVE. HE, TOO, DISSENTED IN THE *TINKER* CASE.

wrote in the *Tinker* dissent. The Court, he added, "decided precisely the opposite" in a number of cases, including *Adderley* v. *Florida* (the student protest case cited by school board attorney Allan Herrick).

According to Justice Black, these rulings supported the notion that schools—like churches, the courthouse, and the U.S. Congress—were places where people could not spout off about anything at any time. Schools were set up to teach children, not to provide a forum for students, Black said. "Public school students [are not] sent to the schools at public expense to broadcast political or any other views to educate and inform the public," he asserted.

The dissenting justice cited a 1915 case, *Waugh* v. *Mississippi University*, to strengthen his argument. That case involved the state university's ban on fraternities. Students protested that the ban infringed on their First Amendment right to gather peacefully with whomever they chose. The Supreme Court upheld the ban, saying that the state-supported school had the right to make its own rules without having the court second-guess them. In the majority opinion, the Court noted that fraternities might have "divided the attention of the students and distracted from that singleness of purpose" needed to accomplish the school's mission.

The same reasoning should apply to the Iowa public schools, Justice Black argued. "The Court," he said, "should accord Iowa educational institutions the same right to determine for themselves to what extent free expression should be allowed in its schools as it accorded Mississippi with reference to freedom of assembly."

Like Justice Fortas, Justice Black noted that students learned important lessons at school. But unlike Fortas, who stressed that students should be learning about their rights as citizens, Black focused on the importance of teaching discipline. "Uncontrolled and uncontrollable liberty is an enemy to domestic peace," he said. "School discipline, like parental discipline, is an integral and important part of training our children to be good citizens—to be better citizens."

At the time of the *Tinker* decision, the controversy over the Vietnam War had inflamed college campuses. In searing and cynical terms, Justice Black detailed the misdeeds of protesting college students who he said were "apparently confident that they know far more about how to operate public school systems than do their parents, teachers, and elected school officials." According to the justice, these students were "already running loose, conducting break-ins, sit-ins, lie-ins, and smash-ins." The Court, by its action, had encouraged this atmosphere of unrest and disregard for order to spread to the nation's public schools, he charged. By allowing the students involved in the armband controversy to ignore school rules, the Court had subjected the nation's public schools to "the whims and caprices of their loudest-mouthed, but maybe not their brightest, students," according to Black. He ended with the disclaimer that he, at least, did not believe the Constitution required "teachers, parents, and elected school officials to surrender control" of the schools to the students.

John Tinker later suggested that Justice Black may have issued his dissent in reaction to the growing number of protests on college campuses at the time.

At an annual gathering of the ICLU in 2003, Dan Johnston, now a civil rights attorney in New York City, told the audience that he believed school officials had been too confident that they would win the case, and that helped the students' cause. "The arrogance of these people was just extraordinary," Johnston said. "I don't think they thought they had any chance of losing—and we took advantage of that."

SIX
AFTERMATH

THE TWO LENGTHY OPINIONS—Justice Fortas's majority opinion and Justice Black's dissent—reflected the divergent views held by Americans on the case. After Fortas read the majority opinion, Black took aim at the decision in a caustic diatribe that lasted for twenty minutes. The justice—who would celebrate his eighty-third birthday the following week—finished his statements with the words, "I want it thoroughly known that I disclaim any sentence, any word, any part of what the Court does today."

In its report on the decision the next day, the *New York Times* echoed some of Black's concerns, noting that the decision might make it more difficult for schools to take "objectionable" books out of school libraries or control what was published in school newspapers. "Principals and deans," the article continued, "may also encounter legal difficulty when they attempt to discipline student protesters."

CELEBRATION TIME OR INVITATION TO DISASTER?

For the students and their supporters, however, the decision was a reason to celebrate. "It is the biggest First Amendment case for public schools and public school students ever," said Kevin O'Shea, publisher of a legal newsletter, *First Amendment Rights in Education*.

Mary Beth Tinker, the only one of the three peti-tioners still in high school when the Court ruled on the case, found the victory both gratifying and embarrassing. United Press International circulated her photograph to newspapers throughout the nation, and the *New York Times* ran it along with a page one story headlined "High Court Upholds A Student Protest." The decision sent a horde of reporters to her new school. "By that time, we had moved to St. Louis and I was in a different school," she recalled during the online session arranged by the American Bar Association. "I remember *Time* magazine coming to the school and taking pictures of me in chemistry class. It was kind of embarrassing, especially since I had just started going to that school a few months earlier. But in a way, I was proud."

John Tinker said he was "glad" and "excited" when a reporter called him at the University of Iowa to get his reaction to the decision. He later noted, "If we intend to have a democracy, it is important that we teach democracy in the schools."

To Christopher Eckhardt, the case was a turning point in winning rights for students. "What George (Wash-ington) and the boys did for white males in 1776, what Abraham Lincoln did to a certain extent during the time of the Civil War for African-American males, what the women's suffrage movement in the 1920s did for women, the *Tinker* case did for children in America," he said in an article marking the thirtieth anniversary of the *Tinker* decision.

Others also recognized the case as a turning point—but one that led to Justice Black's predicted "revolutionary era of permissiveness." Beginning in the 1960s, society as a whole became less strict. In the years that followed the decision, schools relaxed codes on dress, behavior, and speech. To Christopher Eckhardt, that was a good thing. "Thank God [schools are] more permissive," said Christopher Eckhardt, one of the student protesters in an article marking the thirtieth anniversary of the *Tinker* ruling. "What is America if we don't have freedom?"

Critics, however, charged that the Court had turned over control of the schools to students. The *Tinker* decision, they believed, was an invitation to disaster. They saw a moral decline among students and staff that set the stage for school shootings, violent gang wars, and drug and alcohol abuse. The Court's nod to student protest, they contended, resulted in escalating demonstrations against the Vietnam War that occurred in the late 1960s and early 1970s, mostly on college campuses. Still others believed that the decision, by encouraging such protests, helped bring about an end to the war.

CHALLENGES TO TINKER STANDARD

For seventeen years, the *Tinker* decision stood as a practically unassailable guardian of free speech among students and teachers. Lawyers, judges, and justices cited Justice Fortas's opinion in countless cases involving students' rights. "It really was—and is—the landmark student First Amendment case," said Mark Goodman, executive director of the Student Press Law Center. "It set the stage for all First Amendment cases involving students."

Even Mary Beth Tinker's young son cited it in his defense years later when he was suspended for throwing an eraser at school. The principal, his mother laughingly related, had heard of the case but told the youngster that it wouldn't get him out of trouble.

The *Tinker* ruling set a standard used in other students' rights cases as well. Advocates seeking to protect students from general drug searches and drug testing invariably referred to *Tinker* in their arguments. However,

The First Amendment rights upheld in the *Tinker* case took a beating when the Supreme Court, in 1986, upheld the suspension of Matthew Fraser from his high school for using sexual references in a speech during a campaign for student government.

in the 1980s courts began to put limitations on students' rights.

Beginning in 1986 with its ruling in *Bethel School District No. 403 v. Fraser*, the U.S. Supreme Court has allowed schools more leeway in limiting students' rights. In the *Fraser* case, the Court upheld the suspension of Matthew Fraser for using sexual references in a speech supporting another student during his campaign for student government. The Court agreed that Fraser's lewd speech had interfered with the school's ability to teach "essential lessons of civil, mature conduct."

Chief Justice Warren Burger's majority opinion separated political speech, which the *Tinker* decision ruled should be protected, and lewd speech. "Nothing in the Constitution prohibits the states from insisting that certain modes of expression are inappropriate and subject to sanctions," Burger wrote. "The inculcation of these values is truly the work of the school, and the determination of what manner of speech is inappropriate properly rests with the school board." First Amendment law, he said, recognizes that the state has an interest in "protecting minors from exposure to vulgar and offensive spoken language."

An earlier case also relaxed the *Tinker* standard as it applied to drug searches of students at school. The 1985 case, *New Jersey* v. *T.L.O.*, focused on students' Fourth Amendment rights against unreasonable search and seizure. It concerned the arrest of a fourteen-year-old student—referred to by her initials, T.L.O., in the Court case—after the school principal found marijuana in her purse. The girl had not given the principal permission to search her purse, nor had he obtained a search warrant, usually required for a legal search of an adult's property. Ultimately, the Supreme Court ruled that schools, acting in place of parents, did not have to get search warrants before searching students' possessions. Subsequent rulings sharply limited students' Fourth Amendment rights by allowing mandatory drug testing in schools.

In another First Amendment case, the Supreme Court, in its 1988 *Hazelwood School District* v. *Kuhlmeier* decision, gave school officials more power to regulate and censor material in student publications sponsored by schools. In arguing their case, lawyers for student Cathy Kuhlmeier and the other student plaintiffs relied heavily on the *Tinker* decision. The students had objected when the principal refused to allow the student newspaper to publish an article written by students on divorce and birth control. In the maze of court proceedings leading up to the Supreme Court hearing, the students' case lost in district court, but won on appeal.

Ultimately, the Supreme Court ruled against the students. Justice Byron White wrote the decision for the five-justice majority. In it, he established a new standard on which to judge student expression that appears in school-sponsored publications and activities. According to White, school rules governing such student speech would not be considered unconstitutional as long as the rules were "reasonably related to legitimate pedagogical concerns." Under this new standard, officials could legitimately censor student speech that advocated "drug or alcohol use, irresponsible sex, or conduct otherwise inconsistent with 'the shared values of a civilized social order.'"

Justice William Brennan, joined by Justices Harry Blackmun and Thurgood Marshall, wrote a scathing dissent. He accused the majority of approving of "brutal censorship" and said the ruling "denudes high school students of much of the First Amendment protection that *Tinker . . .* prescribed." The case, said Brennan, showed how school officials (and the courts) discriminate against certain views but hide their actions by pretending merely to be protecting students from "sensitive topics."

LasTInG LeGacY

Even in the face of more recent rulings that "chip away" at *Tinker*'s broad guarantees, its supporters believe that the decision still stands as an important protector of free

T-SHIRTS, TERRORISM, AND TEEN RIGHTS

Almost thirty-eight years after Des Moines school officials suspended students for wearing black armbands to school to protest the Vietnam War, another student was sent home for wearing a T-shirt to school that criticized a different war. Like the Tinkers and Christopher Eckhardt, Bretton Barber pursued in court his right to free speech. And like the students of the 1960s, Barber won the right to express his political views in school. In this case, a federal judge made the final ruling.

Barber's saga began on February 17, 2003, when he wore a T-shirt to school that featured a photograph of President George W. Bush and the caption "International Terrorist." The seventeen-year-old wore the shirt to protest America's threat to wage war on Iraq. A month later, on March 19, 2003, the United States launched more than forty cruise missiles against Iraq in a military action that unseated that country's ruler, Saddam Hussein.

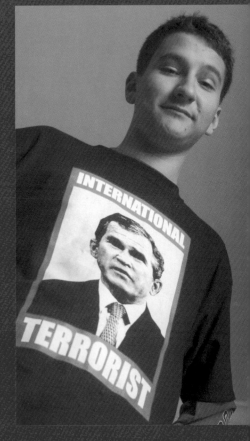

IN 2003, BRETTON BARBER WORE A T-SHIRT TO SCHOOL THAT PROCLAIMED PRESIDENT GEORGE W. BUSH WAS AN "INTERNATIONAL TERRORIST." BARBER REFUSED TO BACK DOWN AND THE DISTRICT COURT IN HIS STATE DECIDED IN HIS FAVOR.

"I wore the shirt to spark discussion among the students on an issue I cared deeply about," Barber said later. "The shirt was meant to emphasize the message 'no war.'. . . I had hoped to generate some discussion about what was then the brewing war in Iraq." Barber gave a class presentation comparing Bush to Hussein for an assignment in his first-period English class that day.

Barber wore the shirt without incident for the rest of his morning classes at Dearborn High School in Dearborn, Michigan, where he attended the eleventh grade. Sometime during lunch, Vice Principal Michael Shelton told the teenager to turn the shirt inside out, take it off, or leave school. When Barber asked why he could not wear the shirt, the vice principal told him that it "promoted terrorism." Shelton sent Barber home when he refused to change the shirt. Later that day, after reviewing the *Tinker* case on the Internet, Barber called the school principal, Judith Coebly, to discuss his rights. According to Barber, the principal quoted from Justice Hugo L. Black's dissenting opinion in *Tinker* to bolster her position that schools had the right to regulate students' speech. "I knew that wasn't how the case came out," the honor student told reporters, "but I didn't argue with her."

Coebly told Barber he would be barred from school if he appeared wearing the T-shirt. He did not wear the T-shirt to school again.

The teenager, a member of the American Civil Liberties Union (ACLU), asked the Michigan branch of the civil rights organization for help. The group's lawyers agreed to represent Barber in his suit against the school and Coebly. Barber also contacted the press.

In the complaint filed in U.S. District Court for the Eastern District of Michigan, Barber's lawyers noted that his actions had not interrupted classes or caused any disturbance or commotion. They also noted that other students had worn similar T-shirts to school that expressed views on abortion, unrest in the Middle East, and even President Bush without being censored.

According to Barber's complaint, school officials violated his right to free speech and expression—and violated the First and Fourteenth Amendments—when they ordered him not to wear the T-shirt. The officials acted solely because they disagreed with the message Barber's T-shirt conveyed, the lawyers charged. They asked the court to order the school to allow Barber to wear the T-shirt to school and to award him "nominal damages."

In a separate court document, the ACLU lawyers quoted a 1972 judgment in the Fifth Circuit Court of Appeals to make their case:

One of the great concerns of our time is that our young people, disillusioned by our political processes, are disengaging from political participation. It is most important that our young become convinced that our Constitution is a living reality, not parchment under glass.

The earlier case, *Shanley* v. *Northeast Independent School District*, involved the suspension of five Texas high school seniors for distributing on campus an underground newspaper that they had produced off campus. The Fifth Circuit barred the Texas school from recording zeroes in the students' permanent records as punishment. Although only a lower court decision, the ruling has served as a model for many other cases.

Dearborn school officials told the court they feared that Barber's T-shirt would cause a disturbance among the student body. More than half of the school's students were of Arab descent and many were Muslim. They sent

Barber home, they said, to keep order and ensure that the school environment was "conducive to learning."

On October 1, 2003, U.S. District Judge Patrick Duggan ruled in favor of the Michigan student. In issuing a preliminary injunction that lifted the school's ban against the T-shirt, Judge Duggan echoed the views expressed by U.S. Supreme Court Justice Abe Fortas in the *Tinker* decision. "The courts have never declared that the school yard is an inappropriate place for political debate," Duggan stated. "Students benefit when school officials provide an environment where they can openly express their diverging viewpoints and when they learn to tolerate the opinions of others."

If the T-shirt causes a "substantial disruption" at the school in the future, the judge noted, school officials can ask the court to reconsider the ruling.

On November 8, 2003, John Tinker presented Bretton Barber with an ACLU award honoring him for his courageous stand. Andrew Nickelhoff, the ACLU lawyer who represented Barber, said the case "teaches that the First Amendment protects our right to express our opinions, and that sometimes we must have the courage—as Brett Barber did—to defend our rights."

speech for students. "The lasting legacy of *Tinker*," said publisher O'Shea, "is that the burden is on school officials to reasonably show that student speech could very well be disruptive before they can censor."

It is an issue well worth the effort, according to John Tinker, now a computer systems analyst in Missouri. He continues to support free speech through his own Web site and other activities. "It's the issue of the importance of protecting the unpopular view," Tinker said. "That's what makes the First Amendment what it is. Otherwise it would just be meaningless."

Christopher Eckhardt said the case taught him important lessons. "I learned that the process, although slow, does work," he said. "I learned also that with faith, and patience, justice prevails." Today Eckhardt runs a tutoring and counseling service for young people and also advises candidates for public office.

Mary Beth Tinker, a pediatric nurse in St. Louis, also works with youth, offering support to teens embroiled in their free-speech battles. "If [my case] has enabled kids to speak up more freely, then I'm glad," she said, "because they certainly need to be heard. Especially now."

TImeLIne

December 11, 1965
Peace activists meet at the home of William and Margaret Eckhardt to discuss ways to protest the Vietnam War. Proposal adopted to wear black armbands on December 16 to express support for extending Christmas truce and to mourn those killed in the war.

December 13, 1965
Des Moines school officials block publication of high school student Ross Peterson's article about the planned protest, titled "We Mourn/Attention Students!"

December 14, 1965
Principals of Des Moines' five high schools and other school officials discuss the students' planned protest and vote to ban the armbands.

December 15, 1965
The ban on the armband protest is announced at Des Moines middle and high schools.

December 16, 1965
Mary Beth Tinker, Christopher Eckhardt, and about two dozen other middle and high school students wear black armbands to school. Hope and Paul Tinker wear the bands

to their elementary classes. School officials suspend four students, including Mary Beth and Christopher.

December 17, 1965
John Tinker wears a black armband to class at North High School and is sent home.

December 21, 1965
Two hundred people attend the Des Moines school board meeting. After two hours of discussion about the armband issue, the school board votes 4 to 3 to postpone a decision on the matter until the next meeting.

January 3, 1966
The school board holds another meeting on the armband issue, attended by a large crowd. After much discussion by members of the audience, the board votes 5 to 2 to uphold the ban on armbands.

March 14, 1966
ACLU attorney Dan Johnston files suit in U.S. District Court in Iowa on behalf of three students involved in the protest: John and Mary Beth Tinker and Christopher Eckhardt.

July 25–26, 1966
Attorneys for the students and the school board argue the case before Chief Judge Roy L. Stephenson. Eckhardt, and both Tinkers, as well as a number of school officials testify at the trial.

September 1, 1966
Judge Stephenson rules in favor of the school board, stating that school officials took "reasonable" steps to maintain control.

April 1967
The lawyers argue the case before a panel of three judges on the Court of Appeals for the Eighth Circuit. The panel announces it cannot reach a decision and asks the full court to review the matter.

October 1967
The lawyers repeat their performance before the full court of appeals.

November 3, 1967
The court of appeals issues a tie vote, 4 to 4, on the case. As a result of the vote, the district court's decision remains intact.

January 17, 1968
The students' lawyers file a petition for certiorari with the U.S. Supreme Court, asking the justices to hear their case.

March 4, 1968
The U.S. Supreme Court announce that the *Tinker* case will be on the docket the next term.

June 1968
The lawyers on both sides of the *Tinker* case file briefs with the Court.

November 12, 1968
The U.S. Supreme Court hears oral arguments in *Tinker* v. *Des Moines*. Dan Johnston argues the students' position. Allan Herrick, attorney for the school board, speaks on behalf of school officials.

February 24, 1969
Justice Abe Fortas issues the Court's 7 to 2 ruling in favor

of the students. In the majority opinion, Fortas notes that neither students nor teachers "shed their constitutional rights to freedom of speech or expression at the schoolhouse gate." Justice Hugo L. Black releases a blistering dissent in which he warns that the Court's ruling signals "the beginning of a new revolutionary era of permissiveness in this country fostered by the judiciary."

Notes

Introduction

p. 7, par. 1, U.S. Constitution, Article I (First Amendment).

p. 7, par. 4–p. 8, par. 1, *Tinker v. Des Moines Independent Community School District*, 393 U.S. 503 (1969).

p. 8, par. 5, Justice Hugo L. Black, dissent, *Tinker v. Des Moines Independent Community School District*, 393 U.S. 503 (1969).

p. 9, par. 2–3, Ken Paulson, "When Symbols Threaten: The Line Between Speech, Intimidation," First Amendment Center. http://www.firstamendment-center.org/commentary.aspx?id=11355

p. 9, par. 3, Street Law & the Supreme Court Historical Society, *Landmark Supreme Court Cases*, Tinker v. Des Moines (1969). http://www.landmarkcases.org/tinker/background3.html

p. 10, par. 1, *Tinker v. Des Moines Independent Community School District*, 393 U.S. 503 (1969).

Chapter 1

p. 12, par. 1, Digital History, Steven Mintz, University of Houston. http://www.digitalhistory.uh.edu/do_history/young_people/voices2.cfm

p. 12, par. 2, Charles Howlett, "Doves in a Hawk's Nest: Viet Nam and the American Peace Movement, 1965–1975, Part I."

http://lists.village.virginia.edu/sixties/HTML_docs/
Texts/Scholarly/Howlett_Doves_01.html

p. 14, par. 1, John Herbers, "Typical Marcher: Middle-
Class Adult," *New York Times*, Nov. 28, 1965, p. 87.

p. 14, par. 3, Jennifer Cioffi, "The Winds of Change and
the Power of Students' Voices: The Student Movement,
the Vietnam Era and the Supreme Court Case of *Tinker*
v. *Des Moines Independent Community School District*."
Association for Education in Journalism and Mass
Communication Conference Papers. http://2003.list.
msu.edu/cgi-bin/wa?A2=ind0309d&L=aejmc&F=&S=
&P=8372

p. 15, par. 1, *Tinker* v. *Des Moines Independent Community
School District*, 393 U.S. 503 (1969). Appendix, p. 67.

p. 16, par. 3, *Tinker* v. *Des Moines Independent Community
School District*, 393 U.S. 503 (1969). District Court testimony, respondents' Supreme Court brief.

p. 18, par. 1, Jack Magarrell, "D.M. Schools Ban Wearing
of Viet Truce Armbands," *Des Moines Register*, Dec. 15,
1965. Cited in AEJMC Conference paper by Jennifer
Cioffi.

p. 18, par. 3, John W. Johnson, *The Struggle for Student
Rights: Tinker v. Des Moines and the 1960s* (Lawrence:
University Press of Kansas, 1997), p. 7.

p. 19, par. 3, "Case Summary: *Tinker* v. *Des Moines
Independent Community School District*," First
Amendment Center. http://www.firstamend-
mentschools.org/resources/ handout1a.aspx?id=13968

p. 22, par. 3, Johnson, *The Struggle for Student Rights*, p. 28.

p. 22, par. 4, Lorena Tinker, "Arm Bands Incidents, Des
Moines, Iowa, December, 1965." Posted on John
Tinker's Web site. http://schema-root.org/region/
americas/north_america/usa/government/supreme_
court/decisions/schools/tinker_v._des_moines/~jft/ljt.
notes.1965.html

p. 23, par.2–3, par. 5–p. 24, par. 2, Donald Janson, "Des Moines Stirs Liberties Protest," *New York Times*, Dec. 22, 1965, p. 3.

p. 24, par. 3, Johnson, *The Struggle for Student Rights*, p. 36.

p. 24, par. 4, Ibid., p. 35.

p. 25, par. 1, Janson, "Des Moines Stirs Liberties Protest," p. 3.

p. 26, par. 1, American Bar Association, "Online Conversation: *Tinker* v. *Des Moines School* Plaintiffs." http://www.abanet.org/publiced/lawday/tinker/home.html

p. 26, par.2, Neil Sheehan, "4-Day Halt Asked," *New York Times*, Dec. 29, 1965, p. 1.

p. 26, par. 3, Robert K. Brigham, "Battlefield Vietnam," Public Broadcasting System. http://www.pbs.org/battlefieldvietnam/timeline/index1.html

p. 28, par. 1, Johnson, *The Struggle for Student Rights*, p. 46.

Chapter 2

p. 29, par. 2, John Tinker, "Excerpts from a Speech by John Tinker at Roosevelt High School," 1995. http://schema-root.org/region/americas/north_america/usa/government/supreme_court/decisions/schools/tinker_v._des_moines/~jft/jft.roosevelt.1995.html

p. 29, par. 3, John W. Johnson, *The Struggle for Student Rights:* Tinker v. Des Moines *and the 1960s* (Lawrence: University Press of Kansas, 1997), p. 62.

p. 29, par. 3, David Hudson Jr., "On 30-year Anniversary, *Tinker* Participants Look Back at Landmark Case," Freedomforum.org. (Feb. 24, 1999). http://www.fac.org/analysis.aspx?id=5582

p. 31, par. 2, Johnson, *The Struggle for Student Rights*, p. 68.

p. 31, par. 3, *Tinker* v. *Des Moines Independent Community School District*, 393 U.S. 503 (1969). Appendix, p. 11.

p. 32, par. 1, Johnson, *The Struggle for Student Rights*, p. 68.

p. 32, par. 2, Ibid., p. 69.

p. 32, par. 3, *Burnside* v. *Byars*, 363 F.2d 744 (5th Cir. 1966).

p. 34, par. 4, American Bar Association, "Online Conversation: *Tinker* v. *Des Moines School* Plaintiffs." http://www.abanet.org/publiced/lawday/tinker/home. html

p. 35, par. 3–7, Johnson, *The Struggle for Student Rights*, p. 94.

Sources for ACLU sidebar, pages 36–40
"ACLU History," Essortment.
   arar.essortment.com/acluamericanci_rmal.htm
"The American Civil Liberties Union: Freedom Is Why We're Here," ACLU position paper (Fall 1999). http://www.aclu.org
"History of the ACLU," ACLU ProCon.org. http://www.acluprocon.org/ACLUHistory/History Table.html
Samuel Walker, *In Defense of American Liberties—A History of the ACLU*. 2nd ed. Carbondale, IL: Southern Illinois University Press (1999).
Alan Rostron, "Inside the ACLU: Activism and Anti-Communism in the Late 1960s," *New England Law Review* 33:2 (Winter 1999).
David Shepardson, "Justice Department Blocks Judge's Request," *The Detroit News* (May 21, 2004).

p. 41, par. 1, *Des Moines Register*, cited in Johnson, p. 98.

p. 41, par. 3, *Tinker* v. *Des Moines, Amicus* brief, National Student Association, p. 3.

p. 42, par. 2, *Des Moines Register* cited in Johnson, pp. 118–119.

p. 42, par. 4, American Bar Association, "Online Conversation."

p. 43, par. 1, Hudson, "On 30-year Anniversary."

Chapter 3
Sources for Through the Court System sidebar,
pages 46–48
The Supreme Court Historical Society
http://www.supremecourthistory.org
Administrative Office of the U.S. Courts
http://www.uscourts.gov
Iowa Court Information System
http://www.judicial.state.ia.us/students/6
There is also a diagram on the latter Web site.

p. 49, par. 4, *Tinker* v. *Des Moines Independent Community School District*, 393 U.S. 503 (1969). Petitioners' petition for *certiorari* cited in Johnson, pp. 123–125.

p. 50, par. 3, *Tinker* v. *Des Moines*, Respondents' petition for *certiorari*.

p. 51, par. 4, *West Virginia Board of Education* v. *Barnette*, 319 U.S. 624 (1943), cited in Johnston's brief in *Tinker*.

p. 55, par. 3, *Blackwell* v. *Issaquena County Board of Education*, 363 F.2d 749 (1966), cited in respondents' brief in *Tinker*.

Chapter 4
p. 61, par. 1, Supreme Court Historical Society, "Supreme Court of the United States" (booklet).

p. 63, par. 1, John W. Johnson, *The Struggle for Student Rights*: Tinker v. Des Moines *and the 1960s* (Lawrence: University Press of Kansas, 1997), p. 100.

p. 63, par. 3, Dennis M. Simon, "The War in Vietnam, 1965–1968." Southern Methodist University, 2001. http://faculty.smu.edu/dsimon/Change-Viet2.html

p. 64, par. 1, Howard Zinn, *On War*. New York: Seven Stories Press, 2001, p. 88.

p. 64, par. 1, Simon, "The War in Vietnam, 1965–1968."

p. 66, par. 1, Elder Witt. *Congressional Quarterly's Guide to the U.S. Supreme Court*, 2nd edition, Washington, DC: Congressional Quarterly, 1990, p. 870.

p. 68, par. 2, Alexander Leitch, *A Princeton Companion*. Princeton, NJ: Princeton University Press, 1978. http://etc.princeton.edu/CampusHTTP://WWW/Companion/harlan_john.html

p. 68, par. 3, "Potter Stewart," Oyez Project: U.S. Supreme Court Multimedia Web site. http://www.oyez.org/oyez/resource/legal_entity/92/biography

p. 70, par. 1, Johnson, *The Struggle for Student Rights*, p. 151.

p. 71, par. 3–p. 76, par. 3, *Tinker v. Des Moines Independent Community School District*, 393 U.S. 503 (1969). Oral arguments (Johnston), Nov. 12, 1968.

p. 74, par. 4, *Terminiello v. Chicago*, 337 U.S. 1 (1949), cited on Oyez Project: U.S. Supreme Court Multimedia Web site. http://www.oyez.org/oyez/resource/case/377

p. 76, par. 4–p. 80, par. 4, *Tinker v. Des Moines*, oral arguments (Herrick), Nov. 12, 1968.

p. 77, par. 1, *Adderley v. Florida*, 385 US 39 (1966).

p. 80, par. 6–p. 81, par. 4, *Tinker v. Des Moines*, oral arguments (Johnston).

Chapter 5

p. 83, par. 1, David L. Hudson, "On 30-year Anniversary, *Tinker* Participants Look Back at Landmark Case," Freedomforum.org (Feb. 24, 1999).

p. 83, par. 2, John W. Johnson, *The Struggle for Student Rights: Tinker v. Des Moine and the 1960s*. Lawrence: University Press of Kansas, 1997, p. 166.

p. 88, par. 1–p. 91, par. 2, *Tinker v. Des Moines Independent Community School District*, 393 U.S. 503 (1969).

p. 90, par. 5, *Keyishian v. Board of Regents*, 385 U.S. 589 (1967).

p. 91, par. 4, Justice Potter Stewart concurrence, *Tinker* v. *Des Moines*.

p. 91, par. 5, Justice Byron White concurrence, *Tinker* v. *Des Moines*.

p. 92, par. 2, Justice John Marshall Harlan dissent, *Tinker* v. *Des Moines*.

p. 92, par. 3–p. 97, par. 2, Justice Hugo L. Black dissent, *Tinker* v. *Des Moines*.

p. 97, par. 3, Hudson, "On 30-year Anniversary."

p. 97, par. 4, "*Tinker* Lawyer Still Has It—Johnston Reminisces About Case; Talks of Freedom in Wartime," *The Defender*, Iowa Civil Liberties Union, 31, no. 2, April-June 2003, p. 1.

Chapter 6

p. 99, par. 1–2, Fred P. Graham. "High Court Upholds A Student Protest," *New York Times*, Feb. 25, 1969, p. 1.

p. 99, par. 3, David L. Hudson, "On 30-year Anniversary, *Tinker* Participants Look Back at Landmark Case," Freedomforum.org, Feb. 24, 1999.

p. 100, par. 2, American Bar Association, "Online Conversation: *Tinker* v. *Des Moines School* Plaintiffs." http://www.abanet.org/publiced/lawday/tinker/home. html

p. 100, par. 3, John W. Johnson, *The Struggle for Student Rights:* Tinker v. Des Moine *and the 1960s*, Lawrence: University Press of Kansas, 1997, p. 183.

p. 100, par. 3–p. 101, par. 1, Hudson, "On 30-year Anniversary."

p. 101, par. 4, American Bar Association, "Online Conversation: *Tinker* v. *Des Moines School* Plaintiffs."

p. 103, par. 1–2, *Bethel School District No. 403* v. *Fraser*, 478 U.S. 675 (1986).

p. 104, par. 2, *Hazelwood School District* v. *Kuhlmeier*, 484 U.S. 260 (1988).

p. 104, par. 3, Justice William Brennan Jr. dissent, *Hazelwood School District* v. *Kuhlmeier.*

Sources for T-shirt sidebar:
p. 105, par. 2, Karen Bouffard, "T-shirt Fight Tests Free Speech in Schools," *The Detroit News*, Sept. 18, 2003.

p. 106, par. 2, "When It Come to Free Speech, He Won't Give You the Shirt off his Back," ACLU press release, 2003.

p. 106, par. 2, Jonathan Zimmerman, "Let Students Keep Their Opinions on Their Chests," *USA Today*, Mar. 17, 2003.

p. 106, par. 2; p. 108, par. 1, Tamar Lewin, "High School Tells Student to Remove Antiwar Shirt," *New York Times*, Feb. 26, 2003.

p.106 , par. 5—p. 107, par. 2, Andrew Nickelhoff, "Complaint," *Bretton Barber* v. *Dearborn Public Schools and Judith Coebly*, filed Mar. 19, 2003.

p. 107, par. 4, Andrew Nickelhoff, "Memorandum in Support of Plaintiff's Motion for Preliminary Injunction," *Bretton Barber* v. *Dearborn Public Schools and Judith Coebly*, brief for plaintiffs, filed Mar. 19, 2003.

p. 108, par. 2–3, David Shepardson, "Anti-Bush T-shirt Approved," *The Detroit News*, Oct. 2, 2003.

p. 108, par. 4, "Judge Rules in Favor of Michigan Student's Right to Wear Anti-War T-shirt to School," ACLU press release, Oct. 1, 2003.

p. 109, par. 1, Hudson, "On 30-year Anniversary."

p. 109, par. 2, Eric Eyre, "Vietnam Protester Pledges Support for Katie Sierra," *Sunday Gazette-Mail*, Dec. 2, 2001, p. 1B.

p. 109, par. 3, American Bar Association, "Online Conversation: *Tinker* v. *Des Moines.*"

p. 109, par. 4, Tod Olson, "From School to Supreme Court," *Update*, Scholastic Inc.
http://teacher.scholastic.com/researchtools/
articlearchives/civics/usgovt/judic/schsuco.htm

All Web sites accessible as of June 29, 2005.

FURTHER INFORMATION

BOOKS

Baum, Lawrence. *American Courts: Process and Policy*.
Boston: Houghton Mifflin Company, 2001.

Cornelius, Kay. *The Supreme Court*. (Your Government:
How It Works). Broomall, PA: Chelsea House
Publishers, 2000.

Hartman, Gary, Roy M. Mersky, and Cindy L. Tate.
*Landmark Supreme Court Cases: The Most Influential
Decisions of the Supreme Court*, Facts on File Library of
American History. New York: Facts on File, 2004.

Heath, David, and Charlotte Wilcox. *The Supreme Court of
the United States* (American Civics). Mankato, MN:
Bridgestone Books, 1999.

Hudson, David L. Jr. *The Silencing of Student Voices:
Preserving Free Speech in America's Schools*. Nashville: First
Amendment Center, 2005.

Irons, Peter. *People's History of the Supreme Court*. New
York: Penguin, 2000.

Jacobs, Thomas A. *Teens on Trial: Young People Who Challenged the Law—And Changed Your Life*. Minneapolis: Free Spirit Publishing, 2000.

Levert, Suzanne. *The Supreme Court*. New York: Benchmark Books, 2002.

Patrick, John J. *The Supreme Court of the United States: A Student Companion*. (Oxford Student Companions to American Government, 2nd ed.). New York: Oxford University Press Children's Books, 2002.

Raskin, Jamin B. *We the Students: Supreme Court Decisions for and About Students*. Washington, DC: CQ Press, 2003.

Saunders, Kevin W. *Saving Our Children from the First Amendment*. (Critical America Series). New York: New York University Press, 2004.

Savage, David G. *The Supreme Court and Individual Rights*, 4th ed.. Washington, DC: CQ Press, 2004.

Zirkel, Perry A. *30th Anniversary of Tinker: The Courtside Interview, Tinker v. Des Moines Independent Community School District*, 393 U.S. 503 (1969). Digital document. Farmington Hills, MI: Phi Delta Kappa Inc. (Thomson Gale), 1999.

VIDEOTAPES/AUDIOTAPES
Irons, Peter, ed. *May It Please the Court: Courts, Kids, and the Constitution*. New York: The New York Press, 2000. Live recordings and transcripts of the Supreme Court oral arguments (audio).

Just The Facts—The United States Bill of Rights and Constitutional Amendments. (Just the Facts series). Camarillo, CA: Goldhil Home Media I, 2004 (video).

Maraniss, David. *They Marched into Sunlight.* New York: Simon & Schuster Audio, 2003. Epic story of Vietnam War.

Profiles of Freedom: A Living Bill of Rights. Arlington, VA: Bill of Rights Institute, 1997 (video).

Real Life Teens: Bill of Rights at School. (Justice Factory 2 series). Venice, CA: TMW Media Group, 2002 (video).

WEB SITES

American Bar Association. "Online Conversation: *Tinker* v. *Des Moines School* Plaintiffs."
http://www.abanet.org/publiced/lawday/tinker/home.html

American Civil Liberties Union.
http://www.aclu.org

Cioffi, Jennifer, "The Winds of Change and the Power of Students' Voices: The Student Movement, the Vietnam Era and the Supreme Court Case of *Tinker* v. *Des Moines Independent Community School District.*"
http://list.msu.edu/cgibin/wa?A2=ind0309d&L=aejmc&F=&S=&P=8372

Digital History, Steven Mintz, University of Houston.
http://www.digitalhistory.uh.edu/do_history/young_people/voices2.cfm

Electronic Privacy Information Center.
http://www.epic.org/privacy/student

FindLaw (U.S. Supreme Court Cases).
http://www.findlaw.com/casecode/supreme.html

First Amendment Center.
http://www.firstamendmentcenter.org

Freedom Forum.
http://www.freedomforum.org

"JEC Legal Glossary," Judicial Education Center of New
Mexico.
http://jec.unm.edu/resources/glossaries/general-
glossary.htm

Landmark Cases of the U.S. Supreme Court.
http://www.landmarkcases.org

Legal Information Institute, Cornell Law School.
http://www.law.cornell.edu

Oyez Project: U.S. Supreme Court Multimedia Web site.
http://www.oyez.org/oyez/frontpage

Supreme Court of the United States.
http://www.supremecourtus.gov

Vietnam Online, "American Experience," Public
Broadcasting System.
http://www.pbs.org/wgbh/amex/vietnam/

BIBLIOGRAPHY

BOOKS/BOOKLETS

Alderman, Ellen, and Caroline Kennedy. *The Right to Privacy*. New York: Alfred A. Knopf, 1995.

Allen, Edward Switzer. *Freedom in Iowa: The Role of the Iowa Civil Liberties Union*. Ames: Iowa State University Press, 1977.

Freedman, Russell. *In Defense of Liberty: The Story of America's Bill of Rights*. New York: Holiday House, 2003.

Hawes, Joseph M. *The Children's Rights Movement: A History of Advocacy and Protection*. Boston: Twayne Publishers, 1991.

Hudson, David L. Jr. *The Silencing of Student Voices: Preserving Free Speech in America's Schools*. Nashville: First Amendment Center, 2005.

Irons, Peter. *The Courage of Their Conviction*. New York: Penguin, 1990.

_____, ed. *May It Please the Court: Courts, Kids, and the Constitution*. New York: The New York Press, 2000. Live recordings and transcripts of the Supreme Court oral arguments.

Johnson, John W. *The Struggle for Student Rights:* Tinker v. Des Moine *and the 1960s.* Lawrence: University Press of Kansas, 1997.

Leitch, Alexander. *A Princeton Companion.* Princeton, NJ: Princeton University Press, 1978. etc.princeton.edu/ CampusWWW/Companion/harlan_john.html

Lieberman, Robbie. *Prairie Power: Voices of 1960s Midwestern Student Protest.* Columbia: University of Missouri Press, 2004.

Rappaport, Doreen. Tinker *vs.* Des Moines: *Student Rights on Trial.* New York: HarperCollins, 1993.

Supreme Court Historical Society, "Supreme Court of the United States" (booklet).

Witt, Elder. *Congressional Quarterly's Guide to the U.S. Supreme Court,* 2nd edition. Washington, DC: Congressional Quarterly, 1990.

Zinn, Howard. *On War.* New York: Seven Stories Press, 2001.

ARTICLES
"ACLU Honors Three Former Iowa Students," *Des Moines Register* (Dec. 1, 1993), p. 6M.

"Action in Supreme Court," *New York Times* (Nov. 13, 1968), p. 59.

"Ban on Arm Bands Upheld," *Des Moines Register* (Jan. 4, 1966), pp. 1, 3.

"Board Hears Attorney on Arm Bands," *Des Moines Register* (Jan. 3, 1966), pp. 1, 6.

Cioffi, Jennifer. "The Winds of Change and the Power of Students' Voices: The Student Movement, the Vietnam Era and the Supreme Court Case of *Tinker* v. *Des Moines Independent Community School District*." Association for Education in Journalism and Mass Communication Conference Papers, 2003.
list.msu.edu/cgi-bin/wa?A2=ind0309d&L=aejmc&
F=&S=&P=8372

"D.M. Arm Band Protest Upheld," *Des Moines Register* (Feb. 24, 1969), pp. 1, 3.

"Extend Ban on Arm Bands," *Des Moines Register* (Dec. 22, 1965), pp. 1, 3.

Eyre, Eric. "Vietnam protester pledges support for Katie Sierra," *Sunday Gazette-Mail* (Dec. 2, 2001), p. 1B.

Graham, Fred P. "High Court Upholds A Student Protest," *New York Times* (Feb. 25, 1969), p. 1.

Herbers, John. "Typical Marcher: Middle-Class Adult," *New York Times* (Nov. 28, 1965), p. 87.

Howlett, Charles. "Doves in a Hawk's Nest: Viet Nam and the American Peace Movement, 1965-75, Part I. lists.village.virginia.edu/sixties/HTML_docs/Texts/Scholarly/Howlett_Doves_01.html

Hudson, David L. Jr. "On 30-year Anniversary, *Tinker* Participants Look Back at Landmark Case," Freedom forum.org. (Feb. 24, 1999).

Janson, Donald. "Des Moines Stirs Liberties Protest," *New York Times* (Dec. 22, 1965), p. 3.

"Judge Backs School Ban on Arm Bands," *Des Moines Register* (Sept. 1, 1966), pp. 1, 15.

"Liberties Union Supports Students on Arm Bands," *Des Moines Register* (Dec. 18, 1965), pp. 1, 5.

Magarrell, Jack. "D.M. Schools Ban Wearing of Viet Truce Armbands," *Des Moines Register* (Dec. 15, 1965).

Olson, Tod. "From School to Supreme Court," *Update*, Scholastic Inc., accessed June 30, 2005.
teacher.scholastic.com/researchtools/articlearchives/civ ics/usgovt/judic/schsuco.htm

"Secret Talks on Arm Bands," *Des Moines Register* (Jan. 2, 1966), pp. 1, 2.

Sheehan, Neil. "4-Day Halt Asked," *New York Times* (Dec. 29, 1965), p. 1.

"3 Who Took a Stand See Results of Effort," *Des Moines Register* (Sept. 9, 1992), pp. 1M, 6M.

Simon, Dennis M. "The War in Vietnam, 1965-1968." Southern Methodist University, 2001.
faculty.smu.edu/dsimon/Change-Viet2.html

"*Tinker* Lawyer Still has It—Johnston Reminisces About Case; Talks of Freedom in Wartime," *The Defender*, Iowa Civil Liberties Union, 31, no. 2 (April-June 2003), p. 1.

"Wear Black Arm Bands, Two Students Sent Home," *Des Moines Register* (Dec. 17, 1965), p. 1.

STATUTES/COURT CASES/DOCUMENTS
Adderley v. *Florida*, 385 U.S. 39 (1966).

"An Appraisal of the Bombing of North Vietnam," Central Intelligence Agency (Jan. 21, 1966).

Bethel School District No. 403 v. *Fraser*, 478 U.S. 675 (1986).

Blackwell v. *Issaquena County Board of Education*, 363 F.2d 749 (1966).

Board of Directors of Independent School District of Waterloo v. *Green*, 259 Iowa 1260 (1967).

Brown v. *Louisiana*, 383 U.S. 131 (1966).

Burnside v. *Byars*, 363 F.2d 744 (1966).

Byrd v. *Gary*, 184 F.S. 388 (1960).

Cox v. *New Hampshire*, 312 U.S. 569 (1941).

Epperson v. *Arkansas*, 393 U.S. 97 (1968).

Gitlow v. *People of New York*, 268 U.S. 652 (1925).

Hazelwood School District v. *Kuhlmeier*, 484 U.S. 260 (1988)

Keyishian v. *Board of Regents*, 385 U.S. 589 (1967).

Terminiello v. *Chicago*, 337 U.S. 1 (1949).
Tinker v. *Des Moines Independent Community School District*, 393 U.S. 503 (1969).

Tinker v. *Des Moines Independent Community School District*, 393 U.S. 503 (1969), dissent, Justice Hugo L. Black.

U.S. Constitution, Articles I, XIV.

West Virginia Board of Education v. *Barnette*, 319 U.S. 624 (1943).

Web Sites
American Bar Association: "Online Conversation: *Tinker* v. *Des Moines School* Plaintiffs."
http://www.abanet.org/publiced/lawday/tinker/home.html

American Civil Liberties Union.
http://www.aclu.org

"Battlefield Vietnam," Robert K. Brigham, Public Broadcasting System.
http://www.pbs.org/battlefieldvietnam/timeline/index1.html

Digital History, Steven Mintz, University of Houston.
http://www.digitalhistory.uh.edu/do_history/young_people/voices2.cfm

Electronic Privacy Information Center.
http://www.epic.org/privacy/student/

FindLaw (U.S. Supreme Court Cases).
http://www.findlaw.com/casecode/supreme.html

First Amendment Center.
http://www.firstamendmentcenter.org

Freedom Forum.
http://www.freedomforum.org

JEC Legal Glossary, Judicial Education Center of New Mexico.
http://jec.unm.edu/resources/glossaries/general-glossary.htm

Landmark Cases of the U.S. Supreme Court.
http://www.landmarkcases.org

Legal Information Institute, Cornell Law School.
http://www.law.cornell.edu

Oyez Project: U.S. Supreme Court Multimedia Web Site.
http://www.oyez.org/oyez/frontpage

Supreme Court of the United States.
http://www.supremecourtus.gov

Supreme Court Historical Society.
http://www.supremecourthistory.org

Tinker, John. Personal Web site.
http://schema-root.org

Vietnam Online, "American Experience," Public Broadcasting System.
http://www.pbs.org/wgbh/amex/vietnam

All Web sites accessible as of June 28, 2005.

INDEX

about the author

SUSAN DUDLEY GOLD has written more than three dozen books for middle-school and high-school students on a variety of topics, including American history, health issues, law, and space. Her most recent works for Benchmark Books are *Gun Control* in the Open for Debate series, and *Roe v. Wade: A Woman's Choice?*, *Brown v. Board of Education: Separate but Equal?*, *The Pentagon Papers: National Security or the Right to Know*, *Engel v. Vitale: Prayer in the Schools*, *Korematsu v. United States: Japanese-American Internment*, and *Vernonia School District v. Acton: Drug Testing in the Schools*—all in the Supreme Court series. She is currently working on two more books about Supreme Court cases.

Susan Gold has also written several books on Maine history. Among her many careers in journalism are stints as a reporter for a daily newspaper, managing editor of two statewide business magazines, and freelance writer for several regional publications. She and her husband, John Gold, own and operate a Web design and publishing business. Susan has received numerous awards for her writing and design work. In 2001 she received a Jefferson Award for community service in recognition of her work with a support group for people with chronic pain, which she founded in 1993. Susan and her husband, also a children's book author, live in Maine. They have one son, Samuel.